Venus

Also by Diana Cooper

Published by Findhorn Press
Birthing a New Civilization (2013)
True Angel Stories (2013)
Transition to the Golden Age in 2032 (2011)
The Keys to the Universe (with Kathy Crosswell) (2010)
A New Light on Angels (2009)
The Wonder of Unicorns (2008)
Ascension Through Orbs (with Kathy Crosswell) (2008)
Enlightenment Through Orbs (with Kathy Crosswell) (2008)
A New Light on Ascension (2004)

Children's Books
Tara and her Talking Kitten meet a Mermaid (2012)
Tara and the Talking Kitten meet a Unicorn (2011)
Tara and her Talking Kitten meet Angels and Fairies (2011)
The Magical Adventures of Tara and the Talking Kitten (2011)

Published by Hodder Mobius
Angel Answers (2008)
The Web of Light (2007)
Discover Atlantis (with Shaaron Hutton) (2006)
Angel Inspiration (2004)
A Little Light on the Spiritual Laws (2004)
The Codes of Power (2004)
The Silent Stones (2003)

Published by Piatkus Books
The Power of Inner Peace (1998)
Transform Your Life (1998)
A Time for Transformation (1998)
Light Up Your Life (1995)

A diary of a puppy and
her angel

DIANA COOPER

HAY HOUSE

Carlsbad, California • New York City • London • Sydney
Johannesburg • Vancouver • Hong Kong • New Delhi

First published and distributed in the United Kingdom by:
Hay House UK Ltd, Astley House, 33 Notting Hill Gate, London W11 3JQ
Tel: +44 (0)20 3675 2450; Fax: +44 (0)20 3675 2451; www.hayhouse.co.uk

Published and distributed in the United States of America by:
Hay House Inc., PO Box 5100, Carlsbad, CA 92018-5100
Tel: (1) 760 431 7695 or (800) 654 5126; Fax: (1) 760 431 6948 or (800) 650 5115
www.hayhouse.com

Published and distributed in Australia by:
Hay House Australia Ltd, 18/36 Ralph St, Alexandria NSW 2015
Tel: (61) 2 9669 4299; Fax: (61) 2 9669 4144; www.hayhouse.com.au

Published and distributed in the Republic of South Africa by:
Hay House SA (Pty) Ltd, PO Box 990, Witkoppen 2068
Tel/Fax: (27) 11 467 8904; www.hayhouse.co.za

Published and distributed in India by:
Hay House Publishers India, Muskaan Complex, Plot No.3, B-2,
Vasant Kunj, New Delhi 110 070
Tel: (91) 11 4176 1620; Fax: (91) 11 4176 1630; www.hayhouse.co.in

Distributed in Canada by:
Raincoast Books, 2440 Viking Way, Richmond, B.C. V6V 1N2
Tel: (1) 604 448 7100; Fax: (1) 604 270 7161; www.raincoast.com

Text and images © Diana Cooper, 2014

The moral rights of the author have been asserted.

The information given in this book should not be treated as a substitute for professional
medical advice; always consult a medical practitioner. Any use of information in this book is
at the reader's discretion and risk. Neither the author nor the publisher can be held responsible
for any loss, claim or damage arising out of the use, or misuse, of the suggestions made, the
failure to take medical advice or for any material on third party websites.

A catalogue record for this book is available from the British Library.

ISBN: 978-1-78180-385-1

Printed and bound in Great Britain by TJ International Ltd, Padstow, Cornwall

Chapter 1
My New Home

22 April 2011

Today is a momentous day. Here I am at last!

I wish I had a mirror. I can't wait to see what I look like! I'm told I'm small, fluffy and white with one brown ear, a brown patch over one eye and a gorgeous, feathery tail. My grandfather was a Papillon (a 'butterfly' dog, made famous by Marie Antoinette), and my mother was a Jack Russell. What an amazing combination – rough and tough mixed with soft and feminine. My angels helped my soul make this choice and they are dancing right now, celebrating my safe delivery.

Oh, I wonder is the world ready for me?

What do you think?

Here I am!

21 June

I'm eight weeks old and ooh! a lady is coming to see my litter any minute. She wants to choose one of us. Everyone is excited and I feel very nervous. I wonder if it will be me? Fluff went to his new home yesterday and it seems quiet without him, even though there are still six of us.

The doorbell rings and I wait expectantly. Two ladies walk into the room and their angels are right behind them; one is golden and the other is green and silver. It's a very small space and the puppy pen takes up most of the area, so the visitors sit side by side on the sofa. We puppies are let out of the cage and my brothers and sisters jump all over them.

Dogs are very good at tuning into people's thoughts and feelings. Suddenly, I sense which lady is looking for a puppy and that she will choose me.

Animals have two Guardian Angels and I'm told we need them. When I see both of my angels talking to the lady's golden one, I know I was right. So while the other puppies pull at the visitors' hair, leap onto their shoulders and lick them, I sit quietly at my new mum's feet. The golden angel whispers into her ear. She smiles and picks me up and I relax on her lap. It feels good and very familiar. We look at each other and it sounds corny but... we fall in love!!

'This one's for me,' the lady says, smiling. A whole host of angels appear in the room cheering and clapping in joy.

My new mum leaves some money and says she will come back for me tomorrow. I have collywobbles in my tummy.

My brothers and sisters keep telling me it's important to be my new mum's boss. I have to be top dog, they say, and they give me all sorts of ideas how to do this. Oh dear, I like her and want to please her, but they say I have to uphold dog-hood! Is that for the highest good?

22 June

My new mum is coming to collect me any minute! The doorbell rings and I nearly jump out of my skin. Once again she sits on the sofa with her friend, Dee, and strokes me. My yellow angels seem to merge with her golden one around us. They are helping us to get to know each other energetically and it feels safe and tingly warm.

Dee turns to Mum suddenly and says, 'Have you thought of a name for her?'

I prick up my ears because I've been trying to tell them my name telepathically. If they are really on my wavelength they will get it right. Please, please listen. Mum smiles and says, 'Yes, I have. She's Venus!'

Hooray!

Dee looks amazed and says, 'That's what I was going to suggest!'

Of course you were, I thought. I've been telling you telepathically! Thank goodness they were tuned in. How dreadful if I'd been called Sweetie or Patch. I couldn't have borne that.

I'm a special puppy and I need a special name – Venus, the Morning Star, High Priestess of Atlantis, Goddess of Love. That's me!

Mum carries me outside and I snuggle into her arms. I'd like to lick her face but I content myself with licking her hand and she seems to like that. Dee gets into the car and Mum places me carefully on Dee's lap, then slides into the driving seat.

Mum calls in Archangel Michael to protect us on the journey and a deep blue light shimmers round the car. So that's what the blue light is! I've seen it sometimes hovering around one of us puppies or around a person. There really are archangels. That's cool!

We drive home carefully and Mum seems very pleased to have me and I'm pleased to have her – so far.

I sleep in a little basket by Mum's bed and every so often she leans down and strokes my ears. She says this is my bed but my aim is to sleep on her bed. One day I will. My angels know I'm safe so they are waiting and watching quietly on the other side of the room. They say their task is to stay near me and observe, unless I need help or ask for it.

23 June

Very early in the morning Mum brings me downstairs and puts me outside on the soft grass. It's getting light and the birds are singing the dawn chorus. My angels communicate that each morning the archangels give the birds messages about nature and cosmic energies, and they sing them in for the day. In ancient times the people and animals understood this information but now the daily cosmic news only touches us unconsciously.

While Mum and I sit on the swinging seat in the garden, I lie on her lap and we watch the sunrise and enjoy the peace of nature until other people start to stir at 7 a.m. This is true Zen contentment. Perhaps I'm to be a type of Buddhist contemplative canine, spreading peace wherever I go.

Zen contentment

Mum introduces me to the postman. He's squat and podgy and wears blue shorts. I can tell he doesn't believe in angels because they can't get close to him at all. Mum carries me over to him and he strokes me, but instinctively I don't like him. I tell her this with my pathetically small bark but she says, 'I hope you'll be friends.' She must be crazy.

The podgy postman touches me gingerly and says in a nasal voice, 'Nice girl.' I can smell that he's scared of dogs.

My angels know I don't like him and try to tell me that we should love our enemies. I quite agree with them – I'll love all my enemies except this one. That's my free will on Earth. Forget about love and light, perhaps I'll be a warrior dog.

Strangely enough, I haven't missed my brothers and sisters. Mum and I are cuddling or playing all the time. I make her laugh and she thinks I'm wonderful, a perfect pooch. (Of course, she's right!)

She tells me to ask my Guardian Angels when I need help and they'll assist me, if it's for my highest good. I tell Mum telepathically that I saw a golden angel with her and a green and silver one with Dee when they came to see me for the first time. 'Ah, you are a special dog! You're psychic!' she exclaims.

'You were seeing our Guardian Angels. All humans have one who looks after them.'

Oh, I'm only a few weeks old and already I realize that this world is an amazing place.

Afternoon

I'm looking forward to meeting Brutus, the cat. He belongs to Mum's lodger Elisabeth and, apparently, he's very big. I hope we'll be friends.

24 June

Whew, I've seen Brutus walking across the lawn. And he's not very big – he's huge and terrifying. Think of a tiger with burning eyes and scale it down to wildcat size. Elisabeth, Mum's lodger, found him in France as a kitten, stranded up a tree surrounded by baying mongrels. She rescued him and brought him back to England. The angels of humans and the angels of animals work together to create the synchronicities that bring the right person and pet together, but how can that ferocious beast be matched with anyone?

And what is Brutus doing in *my* life? I'm a sweet, gentle creature. Were my angels asleep at my pre-life consultation?

Mum tells me that he's that size in the summer. In the winter he grows an enormous coat and looks even bigger. Help! If the podgy postman was terrified of him, I could understand it. Apparently, when Brutus was put on a diet, he would rush at Mum or Elisabeth or anyone else capable of opening a tin, clasp their legs with his paws and bite them. I tremble.

Luckily, Mum is with me in the kitchen when Brutus strides

in like an emperor. My angels tell me love conquers everything, so I wag my tail nervously at him and act friendly. I'm hoping it works on this tiger-like creature. At first he ignores me, so I approach him with my tail wagging. He hisses. I turn and run away fast.

My beautiful yellow angel smiles. 'Good dog, Venus. Wisdom is the better part of valour.' If that means keep away from large hissing cats, I agree.

Elisabeth is tall, fair and kind. I like her immediately. 'Hallo Venus. I see you've met my big boy.' She's looking at Brutus with adoration. 'Now you be nice to this little puppy,' she cautions him. In response Brutus glowers at me disdainfully and stalks off stiff-legged, like a feline Mr Darcy.

Elisabeth strokes me softly. Her angel is shimmering pink and gold and is pouring love onto her, but humans don't seem to be able to feel it like I do. I can tell she's warm-hearted and kind, yet she looks very sad. I hope she'll tell me about it. Perhaps my mission is to be a counselling canine?

25 June

I'm sitting on Mum's knee in the conservatory when one of my angels murmurs to me. 'You're a dog, Venus. Your life mission is just to be yourself.'

Suddenly I understand. Of course, I'm an *angel* dog.

Chapter 2
The Battle of the Food

26 June

Mum is feeding me the same dry dog food that I had in my first home. She says it's because that's what I'm used to and she doesn't want to change it too quickly, but it's the cheapest available and I, Venus, deserve better. Besides, this miserable food has a grey aura, so it can't possibly be good for me. The food we eat affects our frequency so, as a psychic, spiritual, angel hound, I need the best food. That's obvious isn't it? My siblings told me to turn up my nose and leave food I don't fancy, then see what happens, but I have a better idea. I tell my Guardian Angels that I need good food because I'm a special dog and ask them to make sure that Mum realizes this. I think she's more likely to listen to the angels than to me!

Lunchtime

I'm starving. Very tempted to eat that dried stuff, but will persist.

Mid-afternoon

Hooray, Mum has given me some good dog food from a tin, which tastes much better, so I eat it all. I won that one. Thank you, angels.

Poor me! I'm starving

28 June

Mum is trying me on all sorts of different foods now. I'm an extremely clever puppy. If I don't like what she gives me I ask my Guardian Angels for help, then I turn up my nose – and walk away from my plate. Lo and behold! She gives me something else. Actually, I'm getting quite good at this. I sort of sniff in the air, wrinkle my nose and look as if I'm being given inferior food. It works every time. The vet says I must not be allowed to turn into a fussy princess, whatever that is. Hmmm… a princess sounds rather fab. Me a princess, angel dog! And all I have to do is turn up my nose at food I don't fancy! Princess Venus, how's that?

Oops… Mum realizes that she blesses her own food but not mine. I watch intently as she places her hands over my bowl of food and says, 'Thank you for this food and bless it.' It's unbelievable. The food seems to light up and, when I eat it, I'm so sensitive I can feel it being digested and absorbed more easily. I hope she always remembers to do this.

29 June

I had a shock this morning. I'm snoozing on a soft blanket in the conservatory when Brutus, the tabby, appears. Framed in the doorway, he really is vaster and scarier than I thought. I don't believe he's really a cat at all.

Life is about choices and right now I can lie here and pretend to be invisible or I can be friendly. I decide it's better to be sociable, so I jump up and skip across the room towards him. When he sees me his golden eyes pierce me. I stop dead and take a few paces backwards. Another choice. I can run away or try to engage him in play. I quickly choose the play path and stretch my front legs, putting my bottom in the air with my tail wagging and I gaze at him, my eyes shining with excitement and hope. He bats me away disdainfully with his paw. Wrong choice! Perhaps love conquers everything except Brutus? I feel quite dismal and leave him alone.

I lie on my blanket again, chanting the dog mantra 'Everyone loves dogs and dogs love everyone.' My yellow angel is very close to me, stroking my aura to help me feel better. The other one is pink and is watching from a distance.

Later
But I'm a dog and I shall go on trying.

30 June
Mum has just slipped down to the shops to buy me some chicken. It's most unfortunate that Mum doesn't eat meat and there are no scraps, so I've got to encourage this chicken-buying. She says there's no point in giving me dried stuff any more because I just don't eat it. Hooray! I'm definitely a top chicken-eating, princess-angel dog.

She's cooking that chicken. I sit by the oven wagging my tail and grinning. She smiles, 'It's worth getting you chicken just to see you look so happy.' I must remember that. She likes to see me wagging my tail. Happiness radiates a positive vibe that makes people want to give you what you want. It tastes as good as it smells. Doggylicious! Not sure if that's a real word, but you know what I mean. I very carefully move all the rice and vegetables with my nose and leave them in a little pile by the plate on the floor.

1 July

Lots of friends are visiting and I know that really they are coming to see me. They all pet me and say that I'm gorgeous! They play with me and bring me toys to chew. But there's a downside to these visitors – they all give Mum different advice. Their angels come too, because angels love to see newborn animals, just as humans do.

Megan comes this morning. I like her and I sit on her knee quite happily – until she says Mum must decide whether I should eat dry food or tinned. Mum's decision! What about me? It's my tummy. Then she says that if I don't eat my food immediately, Mum should take it away! Grrr! I narrow my eyes and glare at her. She doesn't know what's right for *me*! I eat chicken, only chicken.

Mum thinks Megan is a canine expert, so she dishes out my food and when I ignore it, she suddenly takes the plate away! Oh no! What shall I do? I decide to pretend it doesn't bother me.

By midday I'm starving. I hope that my food comes back soon.

My angels are standing back and watching me starve. They are not doing anything to help me. They say they are with me to witness and record – whatever that means – and they will only step in if I'm in danger.

'Hey! You helped when I asked you to tell Mum that I needed different food.'

'Yes. That's because you asked and it was for your highest good.'

'Well I'm asking now,' I growl. 'I want chicken.'

My angels laugh, but in a kindly way. 'Venus, a diet of chicken alone is not for your highest good.'

I want to snarl, 'Yes it is,' but they are angels after all, so instead I mutter, 'Well, what do you mean when you say you are here to record?'

'We keep a record of your choices and actions. It's an animal version of the Akashic Records. Humans are accountable for their thoughts and they earn karma. Animals act from instinct and the right side of their brain, so their records are looked at differently,' the yellow angel tells me.

'But are you inferring I'm accountable for my actions?' I persist, though I don't really want to know.

'Yes.'

I sigh, while the pink angel explains her task is to help keep my heart open.

At one o'clock Mum puts down my miserable plate of food again. I think about the starving dogs in Africa. Then I try to think what my siblings would advise. Never mind that. My tummy wins and I gobble it all up.

Evening

How can I teach Mum to see food from my perspective? Mealtimes are agony. I shall probably grow up with an eating disorder from all the stress. I try to tell Mum but she keeps reading the puppy-training books she has bought. They seem to agree with Megan that uneaten food should be taken away. Who writes these books anyway?

I ask my Guardian Angels to send a friend with food advice that's right for me! Surely that's for my highest good?

2 July

Thankfully Dee comes to see me this morning with her dogs. She says that animals only need love and advises Mum to feed me when I'm hungry and leave biscuits down for me all the time. Yes!!

She has a very small, very old Chihuahua called Chloe, who only has one tooth. They call her Psycho Dog! That's because she barks constantly and won't let anyone near her. When they first got her they had to keep a string on her collar and pull her in – otherwise they couldn't get hold of her. They also have a rescue dog, a Papillon called Oscar. I like him because my ears and tail will be like his when I'm older.

I race round the garden with Oscar, which is brilliant. But Chloe is horrid. She doesn't want to play because she's old, and she growls at me. In fact, when I keep jumping up at her, she bites me with her one tooth and draws blood. Huh! It doesn't hurt and it doesn't stop me trying to get her to run around. But who wants to engage with a silly old one-toothed dog, anyway?

Mum decides she'll ease up on taking away the food.

In the afternoon Tamsin visits me. Her advice to Mum is that I must learn through play. She puts some delicious treats into a toilet roll and folds in the ends. I spend ages chewing the cardboard to reach the biscuits. Mum says she'll do that again whenever there's an empty toilet roll. Great!

Chewing a toilet roll!

At last she's learning the best way to feed a puppy. Perhaps my angels have been talking to her after all.

Chapter 3
Names and Goals

3 July

One of the fun things Mum does is tie long strings onto my soft toys and swing them round in circles, so I can chase them. It keeps me happy for ages and I'm so quick, she calls me White Lightning.

Today, when I grab my toy, I shake it ferociously. Mum laughs and says, 'That's the terrier in you.' The good thing about being a dog is that people accept that you act according to your nature. So they think it's normal for a retriever to retrieve or a spaniel to swim, but humans have to conform to convention and forget how to be themselves. My angel says that one of the spiritual lessons I'm learning is to be true to myself. It makes life so much easier and I like being me.

Playing with a ball

4 July

Early this morning Mum and I are having our quiet time in the garden while our angels beam love onto us, which is gorgeous – like basking in golden sunshine. They tell us how significant a name is: our soul chooses it, and when it's spoken, it calls in our life lessons. This is why it's important always to say someone's name lovingly, so that their experiences come to them in a happy way.

I lick Mum's hand and she sings 'Venus' softly a few times to demonstrate that we have understood. To be truthful, it isn't very tuneful, but the loving energy is there. I'm so glad I have a Mum who will never shout at me, because my name should always be spoken with joy. I feel so safe and happy.

One hour later

Well that didn't last long! Suddenly I hear, 'Venus. Leave it!' in a loud voice. I'm quietly chewing the new flip-flop Mum has bought. It's all blue and shiny and sparkly and it tastes disgusting, but I munch it anyway to please her. She tells me crossly that she has only just got the flip-flops and now she'll have to wear her old pink ones. Why did she leave them out for me, then?

A few minutes later she bends down to stroke me and murmurs, 'Sorry to shout at you, Venus.' But that's not true is it? If she was truly sorry, she wouldn't have shouted at me in the first place. Humans are very confusing.

5 July

I'm having my first injection today and I'm not allowed to go out of the garden until I've had my second one.

I like the vet. She's a very nice lady who lets me have a sniff around her room, which is full of intriguing smells! Even more interesting, she has two lights with her. One is yellow and blue and it stands back watching. That's her Guardian Angel. The other is her healing guide who helps her with the animals and he's blue-green.

I'm observing this when Mum picks me up and puts me on the table. The lady who I thought of as the nice vet puts a needle in the back of my neck. Ouch! I howl and squeal very loudly. It's extremely painful and I want to make sure that they know this. Then Mum cuddles me and both she and the vet give me treats, so I decide I'll come here again, if I have to.

But I narrow my eyes at the angels and the guides. 'Why did you let them hurt me?' I demand.

'You chose life, Venus, and we can't take all your experiences away. It's how you react that enables you to evolve,' the vet's yellow and blue Guardian Angel responds, and with such loving kindness that all the hurt vanishes.

Evening

I've just come back from my first puppy party. There were six little dogs there and I have to tell you that Mum declared I was easily the prettiest and the best puppy there. There were two Highland terriers, a golden spaniel, a Staffie and a great big Japanese Akita. I tried to be friends with all of them, which meant I got to sniff a lot of bottoms. That was easily the best part.

All the Guardian Angels of the dogs and their owners stood in a circle around us, holding hands and pouring unconditional love onto us. Their energy kept everything calm, which I'm glad about as I was the smallest puppy there. We were invited to come back next week for another sniffing party, so I'm looking forward to that.

I'm told that in some cultures humans greet each other by rubbing noses, while others kiss or hug or shake hands. I'm not going to judge them, but I'm convinced that the canine way is superior!

6 July

I'm still sleeping in the basket by Mum's bed. I try to jump up to be with her but her bed is too high. One day, I will succeed and then I'll snuggle up with her.

8 July

We go for an aromatherapy massage at Megan's house and she makes a big fuss of me. She says I'm a gorgeous, intelligent puppy, and who am I to argue?

We go into a little room with a massage table in the middle. Mum tries to settle me down on her cardigan on the floor, so I know that something suspicious is going on. I watch intently as she climbs onto the massage couch and stretches out with a sigh. What? Do they really expect me to lie on the floor while my owner is up there out of my sight? What is Megan doing to Mum? It's clearly my duty to rescue her, so I must show ingenuity and courage. I leap onto a chair and then launch myself into the air like a flying-trapeze artist, and manage to land on top of her. Thank goodness she's all right! For some reason they find this funny and laugh, but after that I lie between Mum's legs where I can keep an eye on things.

Suddenly, I notice that Megan's angel is blue and white and is working through her hands. Wow! Megan gives Mum a stroke and then me. I like angel massage – it's very soothing and tingly, though I do smell rather weird.

9 July

I've done it. I've done it! I've jumped onto Mum's bed all by myself. I had to hurl myself up several times and at last I'm here! She laughs and exclaims that I'm the most persistent dog, so I deserve to stay. I curl up in a ball on top of the duvet right next to her.

I have held my vision of sleeping on her bed and I have finally done it. My angels explain that if you want something, you must picture it as if you have already achieved it. If you do this with enough faith, according to spiritual law, it must happen. However, there's a catch. If what you desire isn't the best thing for you or for others, you earn karma, so you have to be clear about your goal and be prepared to surrender it if it isn't for everyone's highest good.

I'm a bit puzzled by all this, so my yellow angel clarifies how it works by suggesting that I tell her clearly what I want, then affirm that I only want it if it's right for everyone concerned. I must be prepared to let it go if it isn't for the highest good. That sounds like common sense to me. Who wants something if it isn't for the best?

She explains that when you use this approach with the Law of Attraction, you know that whatever comes to you is right for everyone. And if it doesn't happen, then there's something better on its way. It's simple really.

I can't think of anything better than being on Mum's bed, but as I mull this over I realize there's one thing more – I want to be under the duvet with her. I wait a little while then I paw gently at the cover and pull it back. I quickly sneak under it. Mum acts as if she's asleep, but she must know I've cuddled up to her because she strokes my head. I can't help myself. I turn over so she can tickle my tummy. Oh bliss!

10 July

It's early morning. Mum smiles when she sees my head on the pillow beside her. She strokes my tummy again and I thump my tail. I feel warm and loved and safe. This is where I should be. I see my angels are smiling.

Chapter 4

Stray Monster and Other Family

11 July

Mum and I are visiting her brother, who lives in the country. Apparently, a stray cat has given birth to two kittens in his car port and he's feeding the mother. He phones to tell us how beautiful and friendly she is. I'm looking forward to meeting her, especially as I've never met a feline before – other than Brutus, who doesn't really count because he's more like a wild creature. I'm told a real domestic moggy is soft, warm and friendly and purrs a lot. I want to be friends with an animal like that.

It's a sunny day, so we are going to sit outside. Mum carries me into the garden and places me gently down on the lawn while her brother says how cute and fluffy I am. I know that, of course, but it feels good to hear it again and I flop down contentedly onto the soft green grass, ready to have a snooze.

Suddenly, there's a wild commotion and a raging tigress appears from nowhere. She charges across the lawn at me, hissing, yowling and snarling. I run away as fast as I can, squealing louder than a pig being chased by a farmer's wife with a carving knife. (I think that should be blind mice, but this isn't the moment for niceties). Mum rushes after me and rescues me from the attacking monster. I've never been so frightened in my life and my heart is still racing. Is that really a cat? Why do people say they are nice?

For some extraordinary reason, Mum's brother laughs. He says the cat has just found a home for herself and her kittens, and thinks I'm a danger to them. Me? I'm half her size. Apart from a few moments staring nervously at the two tiny bundles of fluff she's protecting, I spend the rest of the visit lying on Mum's knee, where at least I'm safe.

Mum's brother can't think of a name for the cat, so she's called Stray. Stray! What sort of name is that? Anyway I'm calling her Stray Monster. I just hope her kittens aren't Stray Monsters, too, and I fervently wish never to see any of them again.

My angel says that you should never energize what you don't want by thinking about it. Oh no! Have I just done that? Will that creature or its offspring be part of my life?

'Where were you, angels? Why didn't you protect me?' I ask petulantly.

My beautiful buttercup-yellow angel reaches out and touches me gently. 'We did protect you by helping Mum to run really fast and reach you before the cat did.' Then he tells me something really sad. The cat I'm judging so harshly was driven into the countryside and abandoned by her owners when they realized she was about to have kittens. Suddenly, she had to fend for herself and her babies, as well as come to terms with the heartbreak of rejection. She had to become tiger-like to protect her defenceless newborns, and the lesson I must learn is to be compassionate and more accepting. Oh, the poor cat! Suddenly I feel sorry for her. My pink angel sees this and nods.

After coffee we drive to the New Forest for a pub lunch. I'm sitting on the bench outside with Mum because I'm not allowed to walk on common ground before I've had all my injections. Lots of people notice me and say how sweet I am, but a man at the next table guffaws and says, 'I bet he's called Patch.'

I glower at him. Patch indeed! What's more, I'm female.

Mum says with dignity, 'She's called Venus – after the Morning Star, the High Priestess of Atlantis and the Goddess of Love.'

That told him. I look at him smugly and he says, 'Oh!'

My angels try to hide little smiles.

I am Venus

14 July

Mum announces that the family is visiting today. She sounds very pleased and explains that children will be coming. I've never met a child, though I'm told they are small, scary people. I'm cool about it. Surely, they can't be as bad as cats? I stretch out and unwind on the sofa in the conservatory. My angels are relaxing too, quietly observing from the other side of the room.

Children are more terrifying even than cats! The door flies open and two burst into the kitchen, shouting, 'Hallo Granny. Where's the puppy?' Isabel is eight and Finn is six. It's absolutely petrifying. I run to my basket and cringe. I notice my angels are on alert, beaming energy to me to give me courage. Mum picks me up and tells the kids to talk to me gently. They all sit on the floor while she hands them treats to give me – and gradually I begin to think they are not so bad after all.

No sooner have I relaxed and started to play with them than a toddler called Kailani and a baby named Taliya arrive, along with more grown-ups. Oh help! The baby is all right because it doesn't move, but Kailani gets very excited when she sees me. She points and laughs loudly, jumps up and down, then screams. I'm a shivering wreck.

I thought it couldn't get any worse, but yet another toddler turns up. This little girl is named Maya, and she's much quieter and gentler than the others, so I go out and bark my new new-found bark at her to establish my authority. That feels a bit better.

Then I sneak up to Mum's bedroom where no one can find me. Oh Mum, how could you do this to me? Five children – my very worst fear! I really don't think today can get any worse.

It can. The house is like a refugee camp with clothes and toys everywhere. The noise is indescribable with five scary children screaming, shouting, crying and laughing, as well as seven adults talking. I'm used to beautiful silence.

Mum puts me into my kitchen basket and tells everyone to leave me alone, but someone or other keeps coming in to prod or poke me. They call it 'stroking'.

My angels say that everything has a purpose and I needed to experience this disruption in order to appreciate the bliss of solitude. Huh!

After lunch Isabel and Finn take turns to run with my teddy on a string and I have a great time chasing it round and round the garden. Then they slide along the zip wire at the end of the garden and I race after them, jumping up to try to bite their bottoms as they swing along. They seem to think that this is hysterically funny and I begin to realize that engaging with others is what life's about. Maybe older children aren't so bad!

The two-year-olds are different. I bark at Kailani and Maya because I'm getting used to my loud voice and I want to warn them to stay away from me. I may be just three months old but I can terrorize children! Forget silence and solitude, this is fun!

To my surprise, the children and some of the adults are all jumping up and down on a big round thing called a trampoline. Why do they need to laugh and scream as they jump? I lie in the shade of the beech tree and watch them with one eye open, just in case someone gets the idea of putting me onto the trampoline. Detached observation is cool.

Today I have learned that children are terrifyingly unpredictable, noisy and bouncy and that I'm not allowed to growl, bark at or bite the ones that belong to Mum. In fact, I'm not allowed to bite any children.

At eight o'clock I discover that Isabel and Finn, the older two, will be sleeping in the bedroom with Mum and me. Finn is lying on garden cushions on the floor and Isabel is in the big bed. I'm relegated to my basket. My angels repeat that I wanted to come to Earth to experience all aspects of life. Well, I think I've changed my mind.

15 July

I'm woken from deep sleep by Finn, rushing to my basket to pick me up. I growl loudly and Mum tells me off. Me! He's the one who's invading *my* space. Isabel immediately wakes and hops out of bed to join Finn. Struggling to carry me between them, they drop me onto the bed. As soon as I can escape, I dive in with Mum and snuggle up to her.

After lunch two of the families leave. At last, I can hear myself think. But Isabel and Finn stay and for a while I enjoy playing with them until Finn fetches a big ball and starts kicking it. I thought I liked chasing balls, but I soon learn that football is a dangerous game. I keep dodging this hard, flying object and nearly get hit several times. I try to hide indoors but my angels call to me, 'Experience and enjoy, Venus!' That's all very well – they don't have physical bodies.

At last Isabel takes me to a quiet part of the garden, where that hoodlum kid footballer can't reach me. She says, 'Sit, Venus,' and each time I do so I get a treat. This is great and I'm soon full! I ponder the lesson in this and decide that it's to get myself away from stress and go where the energy is right for me.

In the evening the children and their parents go to visit Mum's brother. For some bizarre reason they want to look at one of Stray monster's kittens. I remember darkly our visit to Mum's brother.

When they come back they declare excitedly that the kitten is cute and they might even have it! Stop! I must not energize that horrible possibility with my thoughts. No. No. *No*.

Brutus, the tabby, is bad enough. I'm wary of him but no longer terrified. However, a monster kitten would be a step too far. I ignore my angels, who whisper to me to be open to the Divine plan. Absolutely not!

16 July

Mum and Isabel are taking me to the vet for my second injection today and I'm not looking forward to it. Isabel carries me into the surgery where the nice vet lets me sniff around the room again. I make a huge fuss when she sticks that great needle into me, but she says I'm a very healthy puppy.

Mum comforts me and tells me it's worth it because now I'll be able to go to the woods (whatever they are) and on walks, which sound amazing fun. She says there are trees and dogs and lots of lovely smells. I can't wait.

In the evening we go to another puppy party, and Isabel and Finn take it in turns to hold my lead. Some of the puppies are still nervous, but not valiant Venus! I plunge right in and get as much sniffing done as I can. The people laugh at my daring, but I don't care. When the universe presents you with an opportunity, you should go for it. It's a dog's life for a top dog. I can see my angels cheering! They obviously like it when I'm courageous.

Chapter 5
Meeting the Elementals

17 July

I'm so excited! Today Mum and I are walking for the very first time along the street to those woods I've heard so much about. Wow, she's right – it's fabulous! I keep stopping to sniff the scents on the roadside. It takes so long that she picks me up and carries me until we are among tall trees and bushes. Then she places me on the ground.

Oh no! This is terrifying. Scary creatures are staring at me from the long grass and bushes! I whimper and Mum lifts me up and cuddles me. She says, 'It's okay, Venus. That's enough for today. We'll go home.'

I was so looking forward to going into the big wide world. The angels are most sympathetic and explain that things aren't always quite what you expect. They tell me that I'll soon understand and get used to the woods and then I'll love my walks. I hope they are right.

In the afternoon Mum ties a toy to the lawnmower on a long string and I chase it up and down the lawn. This feels safe and is real fun. The cord keeps getting tangled up so she only gets half the lawn done, but she doesn't mind.

18 July

It's the challenge of the woods again today and I stay very close to Mum with my tail between my legs. She's puzzled, as she expects me to be enjoying the walk. She doesn't understand how overwhelming it is. Why aren't my angels helping me to understand?

In the afternoon I see Mum's angel whispering into her ear. I wonder what he's saying and whether she has really taken it in. But she must have done for suddenly she announces that she's realized why I'm scared in the woods. She tells me that I'm a very sensitive little dog and that I'm feeling the energy of the nature spirits and elementals. She says she knows how to make that better. Oh, I do hope so!

19 July

Today Mum is going to introduce me to the forest elementals. Apparently, all those watching eyes belong to the little creatures who look after nature. Mum tells me that they aren't hostile, just curious.

She carries me into the glade and sits on a bench with me. I see a glorious blue-green angel of nature floating between the trees watching us. Mum strokes me while she invites the elementals to come and say hello. Something extraordinary happens! A whole host of little creatures stream across the clearing: fairies, elves, imps, brownies and others little beings. Mum introduces me to them.

There are dozens of fairies, all about 45cm or 18 inches tall. They are like brightly coloured lights that flutter towards me on wonderful iridescent wings. Mum says that they are the air elementals who tend the flowers, and some of them are fifth dimensional. They look so pure and playful and they greet me in such sweet tinkling voices that I want to jump right down and gambol in the grass with them. However, I sit bolt upright and say hello back, in a dignified way, with my tail wagging. I like them and they like me. One of them grins and tickles my ear.

Then a whole crowd of sylphs flies towards me, all smiling and wafting air in my direction so that the hairs of my tail stir in the breeze. Sylphs are tiny little air spirits who clear away pollution from around flowers and plants to keep them healthy, but mostly these little creatures enjoy flying with the wind. Mum says that she can feel them blowing away her tension headache.

I love the earth elementals, who approach me next to say hello. There are little elves with their jaunty caps, who serve the trees, as well as taller pixies who look after the soil and co-operate with the bees. The pixies are very shy and I thump my tail to make them feel more relaxed. We exchange smiles.

I meet the elementals

And lastly come the sweet, wee imps, who stand only 2.5cm or 1 inch tall. They are a combination of earth, air and water, and they aerate the soil and help seeds grow.

Right now I don't care what the little spirits' jobs are. I jump down from the bench and race round in the grass playing with them. Wowee! I'm so happy to meet them. The woods are fabulous after all. Thank you angels, you were right!

When we are home again and I have snuggled up on the sofa with my eyes half closed, my angels sit on either side of me for a chat.

'Are you feeling more comfortable now that you have met the elementals?' they ask. I nod sleepily. They explain that elementals have never had much to do with animals in the past but that things are changing now. As the frequency of the planet rises, elementals and animals are starting to help each other. 'How could an elemental help me?' I ask, thinking of myself first.

'If you get lost, for example, an elemental can tune into your wavelength and lead you to a path you know,' they respond.

'Of course, that won't apply to me because I never get lost,' I reply, fully closing my eyes.

I faintly catch the angels saying, 'And you can help them by appreciating them.' I fall asleep and they sing to me in my dreams.

22 July

Today I win a point from Brutus, that huge tabby cat. He's stalking across the lawn as if he's king of the world and he doesn't see me lying in a flowerbed behind a bush. I suddenly jump out behind him! He's so startled, he runs. That does it. I fly across the lawn behind him and I, Venus the puppy, chase that mammoth cat. I trot back across the lawn, grinning widely, with my tail wagging. Brutus sits on the zip-wire platform and glares at me. See if I care!

I still can't understand why Elisabeth adores Brutus. She's now sitting on the lawn stroking him and calling him her 'best boy'! After a short while he gets up and strides off, most ungrateful, not even giving her a lick or a purr. I run up to her eagerly for my share of attention and she does stroke me for a little while and throw my ball, but she doesn't lavish love onto me. Perhaps it's the fact that Brutus was found in France that makes her like him? Is he an attractive foreigner, an *alien* cat? But I thought we were all One?

It's strange how you think of a question and the answer is sent to you immediately. This afternoon Mum and I are in the woods and we meet a friend of hers called Gobolino, who is a very interesting goblin. Goblins are highly evolved, enlightened earth elementals with huge, well-developed heart centres. Indeed, he opens his arms to us and a huge shaft of pure love pours from him right into my chest. Ooh, that is unexpected!

Mum says, 'Hallo Gobolino. This is Venus, my puppy.' He smiles and bows to me in an old-fashioned way. 'What do you think of all the dogs in the woods?' Mum asks him.

He replies, 'We are all One yet we're different!'

Bingo! I get it at last. The answer to my question about Brutus… he's just different.

I like Gobolino. He's just over 1 metre tall and has a jolly face with laughing eyes, yet he's also very wise. I believe he strives diligently to clear ley lines and to link spiritual people and places together.

25 July

Elisabeth has received a letter from her husband's solicitor demanding more maintenance money for the children. He lives on state benefits while Elisabeth toils all hours doing any work she can to earn money to send to them. She scarcely eats and looks as if a puff of wind might knock her over.

She still hasn't told us how she came to be in this situation, but maybe she will explain soon. I think Brutus should be more supportive. She gives him so much love and would rather starve herself than see him going short, but he never rubs himself against her or purrs.

I gather the courage to tell Brutus what I think and he looks at me as if I'm a mouse who might become his dinner.

In the afternoon Brutus corners me to tell me that the task of cats is to raise the energy of a house, not to cosset the people who feed them.

I nod and dare to say, 'But I thought cats helped their owners?'

It's the wrong thing to say. 'Cats do not have owners,' he scowls. 'We graciously bestow our presence on people who feed us.' I swallow nervously. I'm half his size.

'But cats are healers, aren't they?'

'Sure, it's in the energy we radiate. But the purrs and cuddles are extra favours we can choose to offer or not, and this cat chooses not to.'

He struts off more like Emperor Brutus than a common tabby. I glance at my yellow angel who murmurs with a smile, 'Cats have egos, too.'

26 July

Mum and Elisabeth light a candle. They ask the angels to help Elisabeth connect with her two teenage children, Annie and Ben. They live only a few miles away, but their father has threatened he will move away immediately to a place she won't be able to find them if she tries to see them. She's incredibly sad. I lick her foot and she raises a smile for me.

Elisabeth tells us she has an older son by a previous marriage and the three children were brought up together and were very close. They always kept in touch by phone and e-mail, supporting each other through the difficult times. but now her husband has forbidden Annie and Ben to have any contact with their half-brother. He won't let them communicate with their grandfather either, so he has cut off family support for all of them.

I want to bite Elisabeth's husband but my angels beam peace down to me and explain that under all his bullying and threats, he's a very unhappy, frightened man. They remind me that at a soul level the family has called in these circumstances and is acting out their drama in order to learn. So the decisions each one makes are the foundation for the next part of their life.

'The greatest support you can give is to love Elisabeth,' they suggest. I know they are right, so I creep to Elisabeth's side and sit on her foot. I wish I could do more.

1 August

I get into trouble today. Some small children are running through the trees and I rush up to them barking loudly and ferociously. They are satisfyingly terrified. Their mother gets very upset and Mum has to catch me, which is not easy, I can tell you. Then she makes me lie down. She sits in the pine needles with me and passes the children treats to give me. I gobble them. Finally, she holds me firmly while they stroke me. They are happy and their mother is pacified. I have to go on a lead for the rest of the walk, which Mum says is my karma for being naughty. Oh, but it was worth it!

3 August

After my success at frightening small children, I'm on the lookout for more possibilities. I spot a mother with two little boys. *Aha,* I think, *they'll be scared of me.* I rush at them unleashing my truly terrifying bark – a lion could not be more frightening! But they aren't in the least bit bothered. One laughs at me and says to his mother, 'It's a bit mouthy, like Scamp next door.' Oh, the ignominy of being described as 'mouthy' and compared to a dog called Scamp. There's nothing like a put-down to take energy from you. I'm quiet for the rest of the walk.

5 August

Mum says she has a special treat for me today! I salivate. Is it chicken, a bone, fish? I imagine them falling from the sky and landing in a pile at my feet.

Instead, I hear her say, 'I'm taking you to the seaside.'

'What's that?'

Later

I now know what the seaside is. I can't believe my eyes when I see it. We walk on yellow gritty stuff that has lots of squawking children playing all over it. And worse, beyond that is this vast expanse called 'the sea'… an eternity of turbulent, grey-blue water with dangerous-looking, white, frilly edges. We stroll along beside it. Mum takes off her shoes and paddles at the edge, saying, 'Come on in, Venus! It's lovely.' She must be mad. Nothing would induce me to join her. I plod along with my tail between my legs as near to her as I can be without actually getting my paws in the water. *I don't like the seaside.*

Then I see a big bird land on the sand. I'm off. I shoot like a bullet towards it and nearly catch it before it flies off. Wow! Brilliant! Panting, I trot back to Mum, my tail wagging proudly. The sand's not too bad after all. I just don't like that cold, wet water. I'm a dog, not a fish! My angel says that you can't take someone out of their natural habitat, and I must say, I agree.

Chapter 6
Falling in Love

8 August

It's a hot and humid August afternoon and Mum pauses to rest in the shade of a pine tree. I take the opportunity to loll on the thick bed of scented pine needles, idly chewing a fir cone. Suddenly I see him – the most enormous, magnificent, hairy German Shepherd, with a huge yellow and deep-blue aura. This creature is a god, I'm just a little dog. So when he strolls up to me, I cower in front of him while he sniffs me. His name is Michael. I expect he's a good friend of Archangel Michael. I notice his angels observing from a distance. This Alsatian clearly doesn't need much protection.

Michael the Alsatian

11 August

We meet Michael the Alsatian again and as soon as I see him I lie on my back and wave my paws in the air. He sniffs me again and I do so hope he likes me. I wonder if I'll dream about him?

His owner is travelling to Greece tomorrow to find a brother for him, a Greek rescue dog. There are lots of rescue dogs in the woods and during our walks we hear some dreadful stories.

Today a man tells us how his Labrador was badly treated before he got him. My heart thumps with indignation when I hear this but now, with his owner's love and care, he has become a proud, happy, handsome dog.

We chat to a lady who has a beautiful Parsons Jack Russell. It's so pretty and gentle, with a shiny coat, and it's full of life. The lady tells us she found it cowering in her garden: beaten, starved and skeletal. She fell in love with it, took it in and fed it. Then the dog warden came to see it and said that no one had claimed it, so she could keep it! She changed that little animal's life and it changed hers. She clearly adores it and it reciprocates.

We hear so many sad stories on our walks. However, there are a lot of very kind people who have rescue dogs.

The dog owners in the woods sometimes talk about puppy farms. Apparently there are people who keep dogs just to breed them and sell the puppies. Can you believe it? The breeders don't love the dogs and often the poor little creatures just live in sheds and are taken from their mothers too early. Oh, I whine at this and lick Mum. She picks me up and hugs me tight.

'Why does God allow this to happen?' I question my angel. 'It's too awful.'

She nods sadly. 'Indeed, it is. But God doesn't allow this to happen. He set up the conditions on Earth and gave humans free will. Then He stepped back to allow people to create their own world, but some of them closed their hearts and chose to exercise their will by hurting animals. It's quite unbelievable to us.'

'Can't you do anything about it?' I feel quite choked up as I ask this.

'When humans pray for animals or ask us to help them, we can and do help. For instance, do you remember that Parsons Jack Russell you have just seen?'

I nod.

'A stream of prayer went up for us to help the animals and we used some of the energy to direct that desperate dog to his new owner, because we knew she would care for it.' I find myself smiling and wag my tail with hope. 'No prayer is ever wasted, you know,' my angel reminds me.

She continues, 'The way humans treat animals is holding back the ascension of the planet and they have to change. But there's hope. The huge portal for animals at Yellowstone in the USA started to open in 2012. It's beginning to radiate a glorious yellow light, which will directly help animals. The energy from it will also touch the minds of humans and help them to understand that all creatures are on their own soul journeys and must be treated with honour and respect.

'Many animals are more evolved than humans. You are here on Earth experiencing life instinctively through your right brain and your heart, while most humans are mainly rational and use their minds rather than their hearts. It would help animals so much if everyone invoked Archangel Fhelyai, the Angel of Animals, and asked his angels to watch over every single creature in the world.' She pauses.

'By the way,' she smiles now, 'the Angel of Animals radiates exactly the same shade of yellow as the Yellowstone portal.'

Mum and I imagine a golden, sunny yellow touching all the animals in the world and we feel much happier.

13 August

I have always understood that the woods belong to me and that I generously allow other dogs to share them with me. Today two black miniature poodles bark at me, so I run straight back to Mum. Why are they so mean? I wish my Alsatian friend, Michael, was here; he'd see them off for me. I shout after them, 'These are my woods, so there!'

And the cheeky things respond, 'No they're not. They're our woods and we let you walk here.' I know they're wrong and they are just saying that, but I still feel frustrated.

Another thing about me: I'm the fastest runner in the woods. You have no idea how nippy and quick I am. I race up to all the big dogs and everyone thinks I'm brave, but Mum says I'm a naïve puppy and I should be more respectful. Then she says some devastating words: 'These woods belong to everyone, Venus.'

'What? You must be wrong. Surely they belong to me!' I respond.

My angel adds in a gentle whisper. 'No one owns nature. It's for everyone… the birds, the butterflies, the bees, all the animals… and people.'

Oh!

I'm such a fast runner. I race up to a black Labrador and sniff its bottom and then run back to Mum very quickly. Then I do the same thing to a spaniel. It's great to be a sprinter and no one can catch me. I'm the fastest dog in the world!

Oh my goodness, a terrifying thing has just happened. I sneak up to a thin, half-starved looking dog to sniff it, knowing I'll have loads of time to run back to safety, but it spins round and charges after me. It bounces right over me and I squeal with terror. I only just reach Mum in time. My heart's thumping, my confidence is shattered. Can it be that I'm not the fastest dog in the forest, after all? Mum picks me up and cuddles me. She says I'm a great runner for my size, but that there are dogs with very long legs specially designed for speed, and I've just encountered one – it's a greyhound.

I'm deflated for a moment, but my angel touches my paw gently and reminds me that I'm part terrier and I can sniff out rabbits better than any Daddy Long-legs dog. She says every animal has its own special qualities.

16 August

What delight! I see Michael and his owner further along the path and I run towards him with my tail wagging joyfully. But there's another dog with them, the Greek rescue mongrel, a big, mean wolf-like creature, though not as huge as Michael.

As I get nearer I can tell that the new animal doesn't like me. He growls menacingly and in a desperate move I throw myself onto my back and slither under Michael from quite a distance. Apparently, he looks rather surprised! Then the Greek rescue mutt, who's called Jack, tries to get at me, growling and barking. But my wonderful Michael puffs out his fur and makes himself enormous to protect me. He barks at Jack, an unexpectedly rich, deep warning sound, and sees him off. Oh thank you, Michael, my rescuer!

Michael has a bright blue light around him. My angel says it's because he's connected to Archangel Michael, the mighty archangel of strength and protection. I was right.

18 August

I'm grateful that Mum doesn't call me funny names. We meet a dog whose Mum is calling it Puffy Wuffy and Woo-woo Bear. I'm cringing inside, but the dog says she's used to it and it doesn't bother her any more. It would bother me!

19 August

It's hot again today and we get up early to go into the forest to hunt again. Well, I'll be the one hunting. I love to pursue anything that moves. I race everywhere like lightening while Mum merely meanders. Sometimes she looks round to check that no one is around, then she jogs a little way, panting and puffing. It's pathetic really! As for White Lightning Venus, I'm sure I'll soon be so fast I'll catch a squirrel.

22 August

Mum's grandchildren, Kailani and Taliya, are coming today and I must say that children are much easier to cope with when there are only one or two of them, especially if one is a baby. Mum and Kailani play in the sandpit, so I lie in the shade near them. None of us notices Brutus watching from behind a tree. Suddenly, claws outstretched and tail twitching, he leaps across the sandpit and grabs a mouse that is hiding in a plant, and runs off with it. Wow! I never even saw it. Kailani is thrilled. She keeps repeating in an excited voice, 'Brutus gobble mouse!'

But hang on! That cat didn't even chase the mouse. As a terrier, I thought running fast was the only way to catch something. Maybe my way isn't the only way to do things? Perhaps sometimes there's another way?

24 August

As we come out of our drive today, we see Michael and that Greek rescue mongrel walking past on their way to the woods. They spot me and nearly pull their owner over as they swivel round to try to reach me. They are so strong, she simply can't hold them back. When they reach me, I slither underneath Michael, my hero. I don't understand why Mum thinks that's funny.

Michael seems to think he has to protect me and he refuses to move. His owner can't budge him. I feel quite safe and happy under him, but eventually Mum pulls me unceremoniously out and we walk on ahead.

When we reach the forest she lets me off the lead and says, 'There you go Eeny Veeny!' I cringe and hope Michael doesn't hear. I'm not Eeny Veeny. *I am Venus.*

A little cluster of kind fairies observes my distressed and battered ego, so they sing my name with love. 'Venus we love you. Venus we love you.' The vibration flows over me like honey and I soon feel soothed and loved. The world is a wonderful place again!

Chapter 7

The New Lodger

2 September

It has been a long hot summer and I've played in the garden every day. This morning Mum opens the back door and grey wet stuff is falling from a grumpy sky. I put my nose out then jump back in alarm. I look at Mum questioningly. She responds. 'It's rain, Venus. The garden needs it, but you have to go out and do a wee.'

'What? You expect me to go out in that! No way.' I stand solidly inside the door and cannot be persuaded to budge. In the end she carries me out into the torrent and puts me down on the lawn where I reluctantly and hastily do what I have to do and run back indoors again, drenched.

Mum seems positively cheerful and says that we must be grateful for the deluge. Not only is it watering the plants, it's filling up the reservoirs with drinking water and cleansing the area of lower vibrations. She holds up her hands and blesses the falling water, then with her finger draws a five-pointed star in the air with a circle around it. To my amazement the water becomes silvery and twinkly – it's beautiful to watch as it lights up and glows.

Just when I'm feeling safe, Mum pulls on Wellington boots and a mac with a hood, gets out my lead and expects to take me out for a walk. In this? Unbelievable. I put on my most miserable expression while she half drags me down the path. A veritable stream is splashing off me. At last she says, 'Walks are meant to be fun, Venus. If you really don't want to go, let's get back indoors.'

Thank goodness.

Sometimes you have to insist on doing what is best for you.

3 September

Mum says that I make her laugh, but really she's the one who is funny. This morning she says she has to do some yoga practice – whatever that is – before she goes downstairs. She lies on the floor on her back and is performing strange contortions with her legs.

I crawl to the edge of the bed and peep over to watch her. She can only see my ears and eyes as I stare down at her. Apparently this is amusing and she starts to giggle. Then she circles her arms on the ground. That is too much for me. I jump off the bed and run after them, trying to lick her hands as they move. Clearly, this is a new game and I'm meant to participate, but she seems to disagree and tries to push me away. She soon gives that up and gets onto her hands and knees to do the cat pose! The *cat*! I leap onto her back and she collapses laughing and says it's impossible to do yoga with me around.

I peep down at Mum

Evening

No wonder she was doing some exercises this morning. This evening she has brought me to her yoga class. It's the first session after the summer holidays. When they see me everyone says, 'Aah! Isn't she gorgeous!' and they all stroke me. I smile and graciously accept the adulation.

Mum eases me into my travel carrier while the yoga participants all spread out mats and sit on them. I observe them holding some of the weird positions that Mum was attempting this morning. Soon my eyelids start to close with boredom, so I stretch out and go to sleep. When I wake up, the room is quite dark and everyone is sitting cross-legged, with their eyes closed. My eyes fly open wide in astonishment. Everyone is surrounded in beautiful shining light, mostly light blue and lilac or gold. It's shimmering around them and is quite breathtaking. Wow, if that's what yoga does, I'm going to practise with Mum.

5 September

Mum is stuck into those puppy-training books again. Oh dear. That feels ominous. She keeps putting the book of the moment down and scrutinizing me. I rest my paw on her knee and cock my head to one side so that she laughs, but then she resumes her reading and comments, 'I have to learn how to discipline you so that you grow up to be an obedient dog. Spiritual discipline is the basis for a happy life.'

My angels nod approvingly. Oh no!

6 September

A friend asks if a young man she knows can stay here for a while. He's desperate for somewhere to live. I send Mum a message telepathically not to be a rescuer, but she ignores me. Her angel is whispering into her ear, though she's not listening.

She says blithely, 'Of course, there's plenty of room.' She's sure the universe must want her to help him.

Her angel is shaking her head. Has Mum forgotten that victims always end up punishing the person who rescues them? What are we setting ourselves up for, I wonder?

10 September

The new lodger arrives – a short, cheeky 'wide boy', though he's no youngster. He rushes in like a tornado, boasts he's a brilliant healer and proclaims to Mum and Elisabeth, 'If you've got anything wrong with you, I'll heal you. I'll bring your frequency up!' They look at each other and somehow avoid replying.

But he does have a saving grace: he really likes me.

11 September

You won't believe what happens this morning. The new lodger makes a fuss of me, then suggests to Mum, 'I'll give you a game of table tennis.'

'Okay,' she replies.

The new lodger says, 'Of course, it'll be a bit boring for me because you won't get a point off me.'

I look at Mum. Her jaw has tightened, but she smiles blandly. They play three games and she wipes the floor with him.

Then do you know what? I can hardly believe it. He shrugs and sniggers, 'To tell the truth I didn't think an old lady could move that fast.'

I nip behind a chair and watch. Again Mum says nothing, though there are daggers in her aura. *What restraint*, I think and assume that is the end of the matter.

12 September

Mum and the new lodger are in the kitchen. He says to her. 'I've been thinking about joining a table tennis club, so we could play together.'

Hmmm, I think, ears cocked.

'But I thought if I did, I'd soon be much better than you. Then you wouldn't be able to give me a game and it wouldn't be any fun for me.' Mum is totally silent, which is unusual. There's nothing like arrogance to create a frost in the air.

Later she strokes me quietly, 'I'm trying very hard to be open-minded about the new lodger, Venus. I'm sending him unconditional love and blessing him.' I give her a sympathetic lick. She would be better to send him packing.

14 September

Megan, the aromatherapist and dog guru (in Mum's opinion), comes for coffee. This time her advice is that after my morning walk I must be left in a cage for an hour to get used to being on my own. She even says that I should sleep downstairs in this cage thing and not be let out until the morning. Grrr again! She has a dog who lives in the kitchen and doesn't go into the sitting room. I've got to make sure that doesn't happen to me.

In the afternoon Mum goes shopping to buy a cage and she puts it up in the kitchen. She throws a treat into it. I nip in and grab it, then run in and out all afternoon. It's quite a fun place.

At bedtime Mum lures me into the cage, but when I turn to go out, the door is shut! Is this a joke? I rattle the lock and whine. After half an hour Mum says she can't bear it any longer. She phones Megan who says she must persevere. Surely not overnight?

15 September

Yes, I'm in the cage *all night*. It's like a prison. I rattle the lock and paw at the bars, and Mum comes down several times to check on me but she doesn't let me out. This is terrible. I wish the angels would tell me what to do, but they are observing silently.

17 September

I was just manoeuvring into top-dog position and now Mum's ruining it all. It's another day of food removal and short, horrid periods of imprisonment in the cage. Nevertheless, I don't let up for a moment with the rattling and whining. I can tell Mum hates it, too, so I'm sure I'll wear her down soon.

The darkest hour is before the dawn they say and it's true. The most dreadful thing happens tonight. I'm put in my cage in the kitchen and I whine and bark. The kitchen is right under the new lodger's bedroom. He comes down to tell me off. The noise I make even wakes Mum, who hurries downstairs, too. The new lodger says to me, 'I've had enough of you. I'm putting you in the garage.' And he picks the cage up and swaggers with it to the garage. Mum follows rather reluctantly with me. He puts me in the cage and I whimper. It's cold and frightening and lonely in here and I'm not used to it.

Mum says, 'You'll be all right, Venus. I'll see you in the morning.' She leaves me and goes back to bed.

And then something really terrifying happens. The new lodger puts big cardboard sheets around the cage. It becomes pitch dark and airless, like a prison cave. I creep into the corner and make myself small. I want to die.

18 September

Mum comes down early looking as if she hasn't slept a wink and rushes straight to the garage. I hear her but I think I must be such a bad puppy that I cringe in the corner and don't move. She opens the cage door, calling me. Eventually I crawl out on my tummy, looking piteous. Mum is distraught. She cuddles me and says nothing like that will ever happen to me again. She's furious about the cardboard and cross with herself for letting me be put in the garage. She takes me into the garden and we sit and cuddle, but I still have that cold feeling inside me.

After breakfast Mum takes down the cage and puts it away. 'From now you sleep in my room,' she says. I lick her gratefully and we go straight out for a lovely long walk in the forest. I jump over ditches and bark at squirrels. My inner sun is shining again.

21 September

Once again Mum is reading those darned books on puppy training. She announces, 'Venus, this book says I have to eat first and feed you afterwards. You have to sit and wait.' Oh what will today hold in the name of discipline?

It's six o'clock and I haven't had my supper yet. Mum is munching away at her food and I stare so hard at her she says it makes her feel uncomfortable. Good! At least that's a sign I'm breaking down her resistance.

22 September

The stupid dog-training book reminds her that if I don't eat my food immediately, it should be taken away. I thought I'd won that one ages ago, but here we go again. The thing is I'm a sensitive dog and I like quiet during my meals. With my delicate constitution I can't be expected to consume food when there are people around. I like to wait until the kitchen is empty and then I can eat in peace.

After all, Mum keeps saying food represents nourishment and an offering of life from the universe, so it must be treated with respect.

23 September

Today, Mum reads that she should be able to take my food away from me while I'm eating, to show I'm below her in the pecking order! She exclaims aloud, 'How crazy can you get!' and I heave a sigh of relief. Thank goodness she won't be inflicting that on me. I'd like to show that writer where she is in the pecking order!

But there's more. Next, the book declares that if the doorbell rings Mum has to answer it and I must be held back. But clearly it's my job to get there first and bark. Besides, when it's the plump postman, I slip out as soon as the door is opened a crack and run round him, barking. I may be tiny and fluffy but I'm loud and persistent, so he's still terrified of me. It makes my day.

24 September

Will this stupid book training stuff never end? Apparently I shouldn't have been allowed to sit on the chairs and sofa. A dog's place is on the floor. Luckily, it's too late for that.

Instead, we practise doggy good manners on the stairs. Mum climbs up and down them in front of me. Apparently, that's doggy good manners. What spoilsports these people must be! Half the fun is racing past Mum to reach the top or bottom first.

This evening Mum says, 'I don't care what the book says. I'm feeding you first, then I can relax and enjoy my meal. Food is sacred for me, too.' Hooray!

25 September

Mum says the new lodger has never been loved and shown how to live in harmony with other people, so we must try and help him. She sits down with him and asks him about his life. He tells her about his awful childhood and it really is terrible, so she's feeling sorry for him. Then he tells her he has been in prison more than once. Gulp! She's very shocked. He says prison was like a holiday camp and certainly didn't influence him to change. He admits he used to do terrible things but, of course, he's now living at a higher frequency so he lives in impeccable honesty and truth. He tells us he incarnated to go through those conditions and emerge as a great master, ready to go out and teach the world.

Mum and I just listen.

Then he tells her all the things she's doing wrong in her life. Mum and I look at each other. She tries very tactfully and gently to say something to him about projections – how we often see in others the things we don't like about ourselves. 'Oh, I know all about them and I've studied them in detail,' he replies, brushing her words aside. 'But I've cleared all my stuff, so I don't have anything to project.'

Mum hides her smile by bending down and stroking me. I'm sure I see his angel making notes!

Later Mum says to me, 'Venus we've got a big lesson in compassion to learn here.'

I want to say, 'Actually, Mum, you've got a big lesson in boundaries to learn – and not just emotional ones.' He's already spread himself out upstairs. My guess is he'll soon be taking over the whole house. How will she handle it, I wonder? I know what I'd do. Dogs are very clear about setting boundaries. Grrr.

26 September

Some of the children and grandchildren are coming for the weekend. Elisabeth knows them all and is like one of the family. She joins in and is quietly accepted. I can't help wondering how the new lodger will fit in, because he doesn't really know how to relate to people.

His entrance is more interesting than I imagined. Everyone is milling around in the kitchen, so he bounces in like Tigger in Winnie the Pooh, and introduces himself by telling them all that he's a great healer and will soon sort them out.

He quickly corners one of the dads. 'My spirit guide tells me you need to work on your inner child sense of worth,' he declares earnestly. I dodge through the throng and paw his knee urgently. This distracts him while he picks me up and strokes me, allowing his captive to escape. 'Well done, Venus,' I congratulate myself.

The new lodger's intentions are good. He fetches a DVD. 'You'll love this one,' he announces. 'You can watch it tonight,' and he plonks it on the table.

Everyone says thank you very politely. But I can see from the cover that it's not their sort of thing.

His angel is very close to him, whispering in his ear, but he doesn't listen.

Chapter 8

Puppy Class

27 September

I'm a very well-trained pup already. I sit when Mum gives the command. I go to her when she calls me – well, as long as I want to. I walk nicely on the lead, though some of the time I'm impatient and try to pull her (well perhaps most of the time, but that's her fault because she's slow). She tells me she's taking me to puppy class so that she can learn how to teach me to be an obedient dog. She thinks I'll enjoy it and will meet lots of small puppies. I like the sound of that.

Six o'clock approaches and I'm very excited but nervous. We arrive at the village hall. Mum lifts me out of the car and we go in to meet the puppy trainers. They smell of dogs, so I like them.

We sit down and find ourselves next to a lady called Kathy and Buddy, her little white Maltese dog. Buddy and I instantly become best friends. In fact, Mum and Kathy get into trouble because we play together instead of taking notice of the teacher.

Buddy's Mum tells us that he's scared in the woods and just wants to go home when they walk there. Mum decides to tell them about my experience. *Are you really going to tell a stranger about elementals, Mum?* I wonder. But she is. I'm expecting Kathy to look at us as if we are mad. But instead she responds, 'Really? Perhaps that is what's happening for Buddy. I must try it!'

We can't wait to see if she does and if it makes a difference.

My friend Buddy

28 September

A really good thing happens this afternoon. Tamsin calls in and shows Mum and me a game called Find. Mum has to cut up bits of meat or treats, and hide them. Then I'm on high alert to race around until I sniff them all out and gobble them up. I like this game. What's more, it's very good training to develop my sense of smell. Mum has started hiding things in easy places, like under the edge of rugs and on low ledges, but she says she'll make it progressively more difficult. That sounds like fun learning.

29 September

Elisabeth looks so happy today. Glowing with pride she shows Mum a photograph of her son, Ben, who is 15. She hasn't seen him for three years. Her friend, Mary, whose son is Ben's best friend at school, obtained it for her. Elisabeth meets Mary in secret to hear about her son, because her husband says if he ever discovers they have spoken, he will punish the children. She's too sensitive and fragile to cope with someone like that. No wonder he nearly broke her spirit.

Mum asks her why she didn't take the children with her when she left home. Elisabeth says her husband was so intimidating and manipulative that she was at the point of breaking down completely. She couldn't think straight. In the end she knew that if she stayed another day she would collapse. She left the house thinking it was best for the children and that she would see them frequently. But once she had gone, he refused to let them communicate. He threw away her letters, wouldn't let them speak to her on the phone and ordered her to stay away from them. He constantly told the children that she didn't want to see them and didn't love them. She had no money, no home and no support. Eventually, in despair, she fled to friends in France for sanctuary. She had reached rock bottom and it has taken her all this time to get herself together enough to come back to the area.

Mum nods sympathetically and murmurs that she's been there. I look at Mum in surprise. She always looks so confident and strong.

'Why don't you just go and see them?' Mum asks.

'I'm afraid he'll do a moonlight flit if he thinks I'm around, and I wouldn't be able to find them again.'

'Well can't you drive to their school and sit outside to catch a glimpse of them?'

'I'd love to, but they'd feel it energetically and they might see me. It would upset them horribly. I've got to be careful and do what's best for them. Every day I hold the vision of them coming back to me.'

She holds her photograph of Ben as if it's her most precious possession. When she talks about her son, her aura lights up, but when she mentions her husband, it goes grey. Talking of him connects them energetically and great dark tentacles snake towards her and attach to her body, sucking out her energy and confidence. It's horrible to watch. That bully is still heavily corded to her. She's working tirelessly to earn money to send to him for the children's upkeep, but she suspects he's spending it on himself.

Dogs are natural healers and I whine softly to show I understand. Then I leap onto her lap to empathize with her and give her some good energy. The candle, which is constantly alight for the highest good of the children, flickers. Mum says the angels have sent her to us to give her time to recover and regain her strength.

I glance up and see my angels nodding. Elisabeth's angel is touching her heart and one of Archangel Michael's angels is beaming blue strength towards her. There's always so much happening that most people are not aware of. I'm glad I'm a dog and can see it all.

Evening

It's puppy class again and I'm looking forward to seeing Buddy, my white Maltese friend. He has arrived before us and I race over to him with my tail wagging ecstatically. Everyone laughs because we're two enthusiastic balls of white fluff.

Mum asks Kathy about her experience in the forest. I prick up my ears. 'You were right. It worked,' she replies. 'I carried Buddy to our woods and sat with him. Then I invited in the elementals and said my puppy wanted to be friends with them. I didn't see anything, but he was quite relaxed and all his nervousness has disappeared. He loves the woods now.'

Wow! If only everyone understood about the invisible worlds.

30 September

Buddy is coming to play. I keep running to the gate to see if he's here yet, and jump up and down in delight. As a bonus I even get to bark at the plump postman while I'm waiting.

When Buddy arrives we race together round and round the lawn. He chases me, then I chase him. I can run much faster than he can and that's exhilarating. My tail wags like crazy. From time to time we tumble and wrestle with each other.

Mum and Kathy watch and take photographs. They laugh and say when we're together we look like one big, white, hairy dog.

1 October

At puppy class Mum says how mature I am these days, how good I am with children and how I always come back to her. Hmmm.

2 October

We usually avoid taking our afternoon stroll at school-leaving time, but today we go out early and see three boys all aged about twelve, who are cutting through the woods. I think of Mum's words, but the temptation is too much for me. I race up to them barking and then prance around them in circles, making as much noise as I can. I refuse to respond to Mum when she calls. She can't catch me. I'm much too quick. Suddenly the boys start chasing me, which turns into a great game and lasts ages. When Mum finally captures me she's unjustifiably cross and puts on my lead. I hate her! She makes me stay on the lead for the rest of the walk.

3 October

Elisabeth is out in the drizzle, gardening in exchange for rent. She looks exhausted, pale with blue rings round her eyes. Mum and I look at each other. It doesn't seem right. But Mum says, 'She's a proud woman. I can't take that away from her.' So I go and sit by Elisabeth to show solidarity.

4 October

Who should be walking down the road but Michael, the huge hairy German Shepherd and Jack, the Greek rescue dog! When he sees me Michael wags his tail and tries to drag his owner across the road towards me. I'm so excited to see him, I rush up to him on my extending lead with my tail nearly wagging off. Then I throw myself down on my back and wriggle in ecstasy. Michael stands over me, as big and strong as an elephant and there's nothing his owner can do. What an amazing creature he is!

At last Mum says we must go and I'm so delighted to have seen Michael again that I step out fast with my tail wagging. It makes my day. Mum says humans are just the same. If someone genuinely likes you, it makes you feel good and certain people spark you up so you feel happy for hours. There are a lot of similarities between humans and dogs.

5 October

I meet my first horse today. They are big, smelly creatures, who look like giant dogs with long legs and funny swishy tails, and they plod along with people on their backs. How strange! I'm glad people don't sit on me.

Mum sees it in the distance and calls me to her. She picks me up and strokes me while it approaches. The lady rider is very friendly. She stops to chat with Mum and says that her horse is very sensible and is used to puppies, so why not put me down and let me get used to the animal?

I'm rather nervous. I do a lot of sniffling and snuffling and run around the horse a few times, but it just stands there, smelling strange. Clearly, it's nothing to be afraid of – it's just big.

I relax and sit by Mum as she says goodbye to the friendly rider.

There's another bonus. The horse has dumped copious piles of steaming pooh.

I slither away from Mum's grasp and rush over to eat it. Wow! Humans talk about chocolate. This is real dog chocolate. Yummy! I ignore Mum shouting, 'Oh, Venus, leave it!' I bet she wouldn't put down a bar of chocolate if I said, 'Oh, Mum, leave it!'

When we walk on my angels tell me something about slugs and snails. Apparently their life purpose is to eat up all the dead leaves in the hedgerows and this worked splendidly in times when people didn't have formal gardens. Then, after the creatures had munched boring dead leaves for centuries, humans started to plant succulent, baby lettuces and juicy, green seedlings, which are as tempting as chocolate to slugs and snails – not the right things to eat, but irresistible!

Chapter 9

I Meet Kali the Kitten and Wallace the Schnauzer

7 October

We are driving to see Mum's daughter, Lauren, today. I can hardly believe it, but she has given a home to one of the Stray Monster's kittens! What! After that mother cat attacked me? Isabel and Finn phone to say the little animal is delightful, cuddly and very friendly. Whoa! I've heard that before and look what happened. I hope at least they have given her a sweet, friendly name.

Oh no! She's called Kali, after the Hindu Goddess of Destruction, who brings about rebirth and transformation! Is this a promise or an omen?

The children are waiting for us in the front garden. They are so overjoyed to see me that they jump into the car before Mum has switched off the engine. Everyone hovers while I meet Kali who, I have to admit, is a gorgeous tortoiseshell. I, Venus the puppy, behave in an exemplary fashion. I sit on the sofa and I don't even twitch my tail when they bring that ten-week-old kitten to me. We touch noses and establish our relationship in a very civilized way. Then, suddenly, she runs and I can't help it – I'm a dog – I chase her. The children run after me while Mum and Lauren pursue them until the kitten jumps onto the shed at the end of the garden. She refuses to come in again. What a spoilsport.

Isabel has chosen the kitten's middle name, Cuddles. She's officially Kali Cuddles! How interesting – perhaps it means rebirth and transformation through cuddles. Isabel also informs me that she has decided that my name is Venus Magic. Well, of course!

I play with Kali the Kitten

I'm bored with waiting for Kali to come down from the shed, but I have found something even more exciting – a big run with guinea pigs in it! They smell extraordinary and run nervously about inside the cage, squeaking. I race round and round it, barking, while Mum, Lauren, Finn and Isabel try to stop me – try being the operative word. I'm driven insane by these tempting little creatures and dart around like a firefly.

Mum does finally catch me and drag me away. While Mum holds me, my angel tells me that guinea pigs are unique because they are the only animals to incarnate from Venus, the cosmic heart, into which love pours directly from Source. When you cuddle a guinea pig, you connect with all this love energy. No wonder children love them.

8 October

On the way home from seeing Kali Cuddles, we visit Mum's friend Andrew at Hampton Court. They have known each other for years and apparently something crazy is always happening to him. He and his dog, Wallace, a Miniature Schnauzer, are inseparable and go everywhere together. Wallace sounds quite a character and I'm looking forward to meeting him. I hope something exciting happens today.

Their elegant house looks over the River Thames and we park on the drive. I can hear Wallace barking as we get out of the car and suddenly I'm nervous. My tail drops between my legs and I feel a wimp. 'You'll like Wallace,' Mum says encouragingly. His bark sounds aggressively terrier-like so I decide to be very Papillon-like and feminine when I meet him.

While Mum rings the doorbell, I hide behind her, ready to run. We can hear Andrew shouting to Wallace to be quiet and that's a good sign. Andrew, a stocky Greek South African with a wide smile, opens the door. He's holding Wallace by the collar, which is a great relief to me. While Andrew and Mum hug and say hello, Wallace eyes me up and down and I look at him. He's a very handsome dog with a moustache and bright eyes. He wags his tail. He likes me! Instantly my feathery tail shoots up and I wag it vigorously. And we are friends. We touch noses and quickly whip round to sniff each other's bottoms. Heaven!

Wallace the Schnauzer

I cross the road with my new friend Wallace and we all set off down the towpath alongside the Thames. I try to play with him, but he's more interested in sniffing everywhere and ignores me when I run after him.

Then, suddenly, we both glance towards some big trees that are a little away from the path. At the same moment Andrew points that way. Something is going on. Mum is watching the river and hasn't noticed anything, but now she turns to look. A man is lying on the grass under the trees. Wallace and I approach cautiously, sniffing. I growl softly. I'm not sure I like the feel of this.

Two men walking along the towpath stop, too, and we are all eyeing the prostrate figure.

'Perhaps he's asleep,' suggests one man.

'We'd better find out then.' Mum walks determinedly towards him. I cringe. What if he's just snoozing! Andrew and the two strangers are with her and one of them announces that he's got a mouth-to-mouth resuscitation kit on him! How surreal.

Mum and the stranger with the mouth-to-mouth resuscitation kit take it in turns to give the man the kiss of life. I want to stop her so I whine and try to paw her, but Andrew grabs me and puts me on my lead, then phones for an ambulance. He hurries Wallace and me to the road so that he can show the ambulance people where the sick man is. I'm glad to get away, though I keep pulling to go back to Mum.

When Andrew, Wallace and I return with assistance, Mum and the man stop working on the stranger. He's obviously dead, but the ambulance people are not allowed to confirm it.

As we move away Andrew says, 'I knew he'd gone. I saw his spirit leave his body. That's what made me look that way in the first place. He waved as he went to the light and he was really glad to go home.'

Wallace and I look at each other. That's what we had seen, too.

'Oh,' says Mum. 'You might have told me! Well, at least we tried to help him and I'm glad he was happy to go to the light.'

And we continue with our walk.

5 p.m.

We get into the car to drive home. Mum says, 'I told you things happen round Andrew! Are you all right, Venus?'

I want to say that I'm *not* all right. I have never seen a dead body before. I want to stay and play with Wallace. I'm hungry. But I can feel my eyelids getting heavy and droopy, and the next thing I know, the car wheels are crunching on our drive.

9 October

Mum wants the dead man's relatives to know that he did not die alone, that there were people with him, praying for him, and it was a peaceful ending. She phones Kingston Hospital to ask them to pass on the message.

The receptionist responds very abruptly that they have hundreds of people being brought in by ambulance each day and she can't possibly find out who her dying man was. Mum says that they can't have that many cases of people who die alone by the river, but the woman doesn't want to know. She's extremely unhelpful.

Mum's aura has gone red with anger, but then she says, 'Venus, that woman also needs help. She has a very difficult job, so let's light a candle and ask the angels to help her to find compassion and kindness.'

And as we send blessings to that hard-hearted hospital woman, Mum's aura turns pink and gold. Thank goodness! It's amazing how humans can change their auras in a moment by radiating different thoughts.

It's lovely to be at home where I can stretch out in the sun and bark at the postman without any Kali Cuddles to watch out for.

Chapter 10
Birds

11 October

After lunch Mum and I go for a walk to the peaceful lake with my new friend, Buddy, and his mum, Kathy. We watch the golden-white autumn sunshine shimmering on the ripples that spread behind the armada of quacking ducks and the two huge white swans. The latter float to the edge of the water near me looking supercilious. I, valiant Venus, am not scared of a mere bird, even if it's large. I wave my tail like a white feathery flag and run down to the water's edge barking loudly at them. They both lift up their heads, rise up in the air flapping their giant wings and hiss at me! Help! I turn and run all the way back to the car, ignoring all Mum's frantic calls. Those creatures can't really be birds, can they?

When she pulls me from under the vehicle, Mum cuddles me to calm me down. My yellow angel smiles with understanding. 'Birds don't come to Earth to learn, Venus. They are only here to teach, and swans are demonstrating qualities of majesty, grace and nobility.'

'What are they doing flapping their giant wings at me, then?' I want to know. My angel beams love, peace and non-judgement to me, and it takes Mum to point out that they think I'm just a little whippersnapper. They don't appreciate my arrogant barking, so they are trying to quieten me by making themselves enormous. Well, they certainly succeeded.

13 October

Mum takes me down to the beach. We park the car on the road and walk down a long chine (a steep-sided river valley where the river flows down to the sea) with slopes covered in woods. Because I'm strong and fast and agile, I race up the hills and through the undergrowth like a white arrow. This is the best part of the outing before we get to that dreary sand.

I love chasing birds because I have a wonderful run and I know I'll never catch them. It's pure exhilaration. I'm thundering up and down the steep tree-lined banks, feeling as if I own the world, when I see a big black bird flapping around in a bush, halfway up the hill. No one tells me it's a baby crow, so I torpedo up to it – and to my horror it doesn't fly away. What am I supposed to do? I bark loudly. Then two absolutely enormous black crows appear above me like great shadows. They are squawking, making a most terrible noise, and dive-bombing me.

Bravely, I ignore them. I dismiss Mum's voice, too. She's calling, 'Venus, come here!' very loudly but I'm on a mission to reach that large baby who is fluttering round the bush.

Suddenly the enormous parent birds attack me. It's really scary, but my terrier spirit is roused and I bark even more loudly.

Mum hares up the hill, as fast as the poor old dear can manage, and puts me on a lead. I have the perfect excuse to leave with my tail held high and wagging. That pair of crows follows us all the way along the path like fighter planes. It's spooky.

Mum says I must not take on more than I can chew, which is a bizarre thing to say because I wasn't going to chew the baby bird, just chase it when it flew away.

14 October

Several large wood pigeons nest in the trees in the garden. They waddle about on the lawn, swaying like badly loaded boats, and make a mess. But my angels say I should not snigger at them or chase them, because doves, pigeons and also ducks are very special. They work closely with the Angels of Love and Peace, spreading messages of comfort and hope from them. This is why they often try to flutter up to people. Okay, I get it! Taking kids to feed the ducks or pigeons enables the Angels of Love and Peace to influence them. Cool planning by the universe.

This evening that villainous tabby, Brutus, has caught a wood pigeon that is nearly as big as he is. The poor bird is flapping its wings in a frantic effort to get away. Mum rushes into the garden and shouts at the cat, who promptly runs away, dragging his unfortunate victim into the centre of the very thick hedge. We can hear it flapping desperately, but there's no way we can reach it.

Mum calls out, 'Angels, please help me set this bird free.' Instantly they tell her to pick up a large pole lying nearby and thrust it into the hedge. She does this as quickly as she can and amazingly Brutus lets go of the pigeon, which flies free.

Brutus the villain!

'What was that bird showing us?' I ask.

'That if you are trapped in a situation, call for help, listen to your intuition and take action. We angels will help you find a way out of it.'

'Okay, I buy that,' I respond.

16 October

We are going to spend the night at Mum's son Justin's house. His daughter Maya is two and a half now, and a bit nervous of me. Quite right. I may be all fluffy and soft like a puppy, but inside I'm a wolf!

However, she's very brave and, watching me warily, she picks up the string attached to my toy and runs with it. That does it. We form a bond of friendship as I chase my toy for two hours in a circle through the kitchen, the hall and the sitting room.

Then I discover something even more fabulous. There are big, brown clucking birds in an enclosure in the garden. Chickens. I race around them, barking in ecstasy, my tail erect and every fibre of my being quivering with anticipation. They appear to be terrified and that adds to my delight. Naturally, that spoilsport Mum captures me and takes me inside, but I expect she'll let me out again.

My angel tells me that hens are very special – wouldn't you believe it! They just look like dull brown birds to me. She says that all birds come from Sirius, but hens hail from a distant asteroid and step down through Sirius before they incarnate. They arrived on Earth in the golden era of Atlantis to offer humans feathers and eggs and to teach them that it's good to serve. Clearly, it's important that humans learn that, though we dogs know it automatically. I feel quite warm towards the chickens when I hear this, but it doesn't stop me wanting to harass them.

20 October

Andrew and his dog Wallace, the Miniature Schnauzer, are visiting for the day and after our shared experience with the dead body by the Thames, we are firm friends. I'm delighted to see him and we two little dogs are scampering about by the sea. Wallace loves the sand and that helps me to like it, too. We enjoy a good bark as we chase seagulls together. They only fly a little way before they land again, so we can engage in the pursuit all over again. This is doggy paradise.

Mum puts me on the lead when we move up to the promenade, but Wallace is still free. And so I have the opportunity to witness a different side of the macho Schnauzer. A seagull with a damaged wing lands right in front of us and the dog dutifully chases it. It flutters down onto the sand and Wallace rushes right up to it, barking. He sounds really aggressive, but I know that he's begging it to fly away. The gull can't fly, so it tries to run. Wallace doesn't know what to do, but he doesn't want to lose face so he hurries behind the bird, sniffing its backside as if it's a dog. Mum and Andrew keep calling him and he soon realizes that this is the way out of his dilemma. Looking crestfallen, he surrenders to Andrew who puts him on his lead.

Mum tells him that it was very compassionate to leave the injured bird and that true warriors are also gentle. He looks at her as if she's mad.

22 October

We drive to Lauren's house today because she and her family are going to look after me while Mum goes away for a few days. We are waiting in the front garden for Isabel and Finn to get their coats on for a walk when something glorious happens to me. I play a trick! I see the boy next door – who is about twelve and has his back to me – working on his bike. He doesn't notice me creep up to him. When I'm right behind him, I fluff up my fur like Michael, the Alsatian. I take a deep breath and suddenly I bark as loudly as I can, like a burst of automatic rifle fire. The boy nearly jumps out of his skin. Yes, he literally leaps into the air in shock and drops his bike. Oh, it's fabulous! I feel so powerful. My ego and confidence are buzzing. A passing cyclist nearly falls off his bicycle, laughing! The neighbours opposite see it and think it's hysterical. Luckily, the boy sees the funny side, too, and giggles. Mum also laughs, but she scolds me – I can't think why. I have brought lightness and hilarity to their day.

I'm so pleased with myself that I leap onto the kitten and nuzzle her. Mum calls, 'Be gentle, Venus!' Then she sees Kali Cuddles cheerfully biting my bottom and she laughs.

23 October

Mum is going to Egypt today, so she gets up early to take me for a short walk with Isabel before she's collected by taxi. She's leaving me. No! Not with children and a cat! *Please* come back soon.

24 October

I miss Mum – well a bit. Today I'm spending some time playing with Kali. I didn't know kittens could be such fun.

30 October

Mum's home! I'm so pleased to see her. I jump up again and again and roll over and wee all over the floor. She's just as pleased to see me, but she doesn't show it in quite the same way.

'It wasn't so bad was it, Venus?' she asks.

'Yes, it was,' I tell her. 'But it was worse for Kali, the kitten. She spent most of the time on the shed roof.'

1 November

When we wave goodbye Finn says the house will feel really empty without me. Well, of course it will!

Chapter 11

Neighbours

2 November

There are fences and hedges around the garden and the people and dogs on the other side are called neighbours. I wonder if that's something to do with horses? Perhaps people neighed to each other over the fence in the olden days? Anyway, we have a shouting neighbour at the end of the garden. When we are outside we can hear her shouting at Cyril or Horace. 'Cyril, do this.' 'Horace, for goodness sake!' The only thing is we're not sure which one is the dog and which one is the husband. I'm absolutely convinced that Cyril is the husband and Horace the poor mutt, but Mum thinks the opposite. How are we going to find out?

The woman is in full flow with her tirade now, so Mum and I try to peep over the fence to see what we can find out. I hide in the bushes and Mum climbs up onto the zip-wire platform and stands on tiptoe, but she can't see anything. That female is really shouting and screaming, and there's a subdued man and a depressed-looking hound sitting on their patio taking very little notice. But I still don't know who is who.

Mum climbs down and who do you think jumps onto the platform but Brutus! He's trying to catch a glimpse through the trees, but he can't see anything. Then he climbs up the oak tree right in the corner to get a better look – cats are so curious – and at that moment the noise abates and they all go inside.

This afternoon Mum tells Megan about our shouting neighbour and Cyril and Horace. Megan replies that they used to have a little girl next door to them called Phelia. But for years they thought she was called Ophelia because her mother kept calling, 'Oh! Phelia!'

I know the feeling. I often get called, 'Oh, Venus!'

3 November

There are two houses bordering the end of our garden. That yappie sausage dog in one of them never goes out. When I ask him where they take him for a walk, he tells me that his owners insist he doesn't need one. If I see him at the fence I race over, wagging my tail and barking furiously, but he never has any news. What a dull life he leads. Dogs are on Earth to experience things, just as humans are.

A friend of Mum's told her that when she was a child they had a dog and a chicken, who were great friends. They would run along the wire-mesh fence together to the end of the garden and back, barking and clucking while the two dogs next door would race up and down on their side, retaliating loudly. They never needed to be taken for walks and were worn out by the end of the day.

Hmm, I wonder what it's like to have a chicken as a friend?

4 November

The nice old lady next door is called Mavis. I particularly enjoy barking at her whenever she comes out into her garden. Mum always rushes out to shush me, then stays and chats to her. I let Mavis stroke me, but I've never been into her garden.

This morning I sniff around the boundary as usual. What's this? A fox has dug a hole under the fence. Mavis is pulling out weeds in her flowerbeds, but she has not seen me, so I wriggle through the fox hole onto her side! Oh, the joy of freedom! I strut up and down her lawn feeling very clever, enjoying the different smells. Suddenly, she looks up and sees me. I dash for the fence. Oh horror! I can't find the fox hole. She's coming towards me, getting bigger as she approaches. All at once, she turns into a huge monstrous ogre and I race around her lawn trying to escape her clutches. I bark as loudly as I can to call Mum, who runs round to Mavis's side gate, shouting, 'I'm coming, Venus.' I fly to Mum as soon as I see her and she picks me up. I can't tell you how relieved I am.

Then a strange thing happens. That huge ogre turns into a little old lady again. How peculiar! I let her stroke me and I even lick her hand. She's very kind.

My angel says that if you are afraid of something, however small, it gets magnified out of all proportion and becomes an ogre. When you strengthen yourself or look at the fear clearly, it shrinks and you can deal with it. That doesn't apply to me, of course, because I, Venus the terrier, am not afraid of much – but it's weird how Mavis changed so dramatically.

5 November

The neighbour behind is in the garden screaming at Horace again. I bark in sympathy, just in case it's the dog. There's no response. Not sure if that means she's shouting at her husband or if it's the animal, too traumatized to respond.

Mum lights a candle and we send love over the fence to that house and the people in it.

6 November

At last the mystery is solved! Cyril is definitely the dog. I hear the virago shouting, 'Be quiet, Cyril. I'll get your dinner in a minute.' Poor old boy. I imagine his owner as big and beefy, with a round ugly face and a squint.

7 November

How weird! We are enjoying our walk in the woods when I hear someone shouting 'Horace!' I recognize that voice, I swear I do. I race back to Mum. I'm not sure if it's to protect her or that I want her to protect me. We look at each other. 'I thought the dog was Cyril?' Mum whispers. If a puppy could shrug, I would shrug.

A thin woman with blonde hair strides along the path towards us with a brown dog that looks like a whippet cross. It doesn't look very happy, but then neither does she. In fact she looks exhausted. As I knew she would, Mum says brightly, 'Hello, lovely day isn't it?' The woman looks a bit surprised considering it's chilly and drizzling, but responds politely enough.

'Hello boy,' Mum says to Horace, then 'Can I give him a treat?' to his owner. By the time this has happened and I have had a tidbit, too, Mum has established that the dog is definitely Horace. Cyril is the lazy husband who doesn't lift a finger to help and won't look for a job. They might lose the house. She's working all day and doing extra hours in the evenings. Now she's discovered that Cyril is having an affair and she can't decide whether to boot him out or let him stay.

All this time Mum has been silent, just listening. Now she says sympathetically, 'You can't decide whether you want him to go or stay?'

Horace's owner confides that most of the time she wants him out but she doesn't want to be on her own. How sad is that?

When we continue our walk Mum says, 'It shows you should never judge anyone, doesn't it Venus? You simply don't know what they are going through.'

I think, 'Poor old Horace. What a tough time some dogs have.'

8 November

Today, twenty teacher trainers from Mum's Spiritual Foundation have come to the house for a meeting. I bark at them when they arrive because that's my job, but they all have angel energy and shining auras, so I soon stop. They settle down to discussions and are very busy. What! No one has any time for me.

I run into the garden to find some way of grabbing their attention and the universe provides me with a bad egg – a bird's egg that has fallen out of a nest and gone off. It smells amazing! This powerful sulphur pong can't be underestimated. I roll in it and yolk drips from me. Fantastic. They'll take notice of me now.

I run joyfully into the middle of their circle, tail wagging with delight. It's not quite the welcome I expect but they certainly notice me. Mum takes me out to the kitchen, where the new lodger gives me a bath. Grrr. How could he!

But I'm not daunted. I'll find something else. I run round the garden and isn't it lucky that Mum has dug manure into the vegetable patch? I soon roll in it so that I'm coated nicely. That should do the trick. I prance eagerly back into the room with all the exuberance of a puppy, my ears flapping and my tail waving. To make sure I get proper attention, I carry a big lump of manure in my mouth and scatter it on the carpet in the middle of their circle.

They decide to have a break while Mum clears up and the new lodger bathes me yet again. After that I'm kept indoors. What's the matter with them?

Later when the teachers have all gone, Mum sits quietly with me beside her and gives me the attention I missed during the day.

My yellow angel strokes my aura gently, 'You know, Venus, dogs and humans have a different sense of smell.'

'So I gather.'

'You can't please humans with things a dog likes.'

I sigh. I don't think I'll ever really understand that. My angel continues, saying that if I could truly grasp that every species likes different things, I would have a key to universal peace.

'Yes, but manure smells delicious,' I respond.

At that moment Mum gives me a great big hug and murmurs, 'Venus, you are a beautiful little seven-month-old puppy and I love you exactly as you are.'

'Except for manure and bad eggs,' I grunt. I swear my angel winks in sympathy.

I am relaxing

Chapter 12

Dog Neighbours

10 November

Megan tells us that her neighbours have two dogs that are very quiet, despite the fact that they are never taken out. However, a few months ago they rescued a puppy. They leave the three animals alone all day, with the flap open to the postage-stamp-size garden. Here, they roam freely but the bored puppy barks relentlessly.

I feel so sorry for those dogs, especially the puppy. How can anyone rescue an animal and then treat it like that?

Megan is friends with the puppy's owner and has mentioned how annoying this is, but nothing changes. Now they have gone on holiday, leaving the dogs alone in the house, while her son comes in reluctantly each morning and evening to feed them. Megan works from home and is being driven to distraction by the noise, but she doesn't really know what to do. She has a key to her neighbour's house and tries to help by taking the puppy for an occasional walk, but it's frightened of everything and is obviously not used to the outside world.

Megan doesn't want to make things awkward with her neighbour by reporting the situation and she realizes she must speak clearly to her when she returns from holiday, but she feels she must also take spiritual action.

'Good idea,' responds Mum, and we wonder what she will do.

11 November

Megan phones to say that last night she did a massive cleansing of her own house and garden, using joss sticks, singing bowls, sacred symbols and chants. Then she lit candles and asked the angels to resolve the dog-barking situation for the highest good of all.

13 November

Megan phones to say that something has shifted already. She saw Frederick, a man who lives a few doors away, knocking on her absent friend's front door. She went out to talk to him and learned he had come to complain about the endless barking, so she explained the situation. He completely understands that it's difficult for her to report her friend, but he has no such qualms. However, he will first discuss it with her when she comes back tomorrow. Frederick is a very determined man and perhaps he will succeed where Megan manifestly has not.

Megan phones at lunchtime. She reports that it has been eerily quiet next door. Her neighbour has returned from holiday, but she has not seen her to chat to over the fence and she doesn't want to go round and make a huge issue of the dog situation.

Megan phones in the evening. She has spoken to her neighbour. Frederick has already been round to see her. He was quite forthright and she was very contrite. She has promised to take the puppy out for a walk every morning.

'So you jolly well should,' I think. Mum and I visualize that puppy in a new home with a big garden, being taken for lots of walks. 'Please, Archangel Fhelyai, Angel of Animals,' we add, 'Help it.'

17 November

Megan phones. Her neighbour's good resolution lasted less than a week. The puppy is still barking. Even as we speak she can see Frederick walking down next door's path. Oh dear!

Later

But it isn't 'Oh dear'! The angels work in mysterious ways in response to our requests. It turns out that Frederick knows someone with a big garden, who loves walking, has plenty of spare time and would love a puppy. And at last Megan is prepared to let it go. I guess the angels were whispering to her, too.

18 November

Mum and I go round to Megan's for an aromatherapy massage. Now that I'm becoming a big dog, I lie on the floor on Mum's cardigan. Something is different and it takes me a while to realize what it is. Peace and quiet! Megan and Mum smile. When you work with the angels for the highest good, there's a solution to every problem.

Tamsin is bringing Dolly, their new Chihuahua puppy, round this afternoon. I'm glad she isn't old like one-tooth Chloe and I hope she's house-trained. I don't want the house smelling of another dog.

Wow! Dolly is half my size but a bundle of fun. She races in and we take to one another immediately. She's like a whirlwind, jumping over the furniture and around our legs. I chase after her and she's nearly as fast as I am!

19 November

Mum and Tamsin are working on a project, so Dolly is coming again today. I sit at the gate waiting.

When she arrives we take it in turns to play follow my leader round the lawn; then we have tugs of war with my toys. What a fabulous day!

Dolly the Chihuahua puppy

20 November

At last I'm going to Dolly's house. I'm really excited about it. I stand on their doorstep wagging my tail in anticipation. The door opens and... *help*! No one reminded me that they also have a Rottweiler the size of a big black bull. He glowers at me for the half-second it takes me to turn like an eel and slither under the car. I stay there a long time, heart beating fast, peering out and refusing all attempts to lure me out.

Eventually, Tamsin persuades me that the big black ogre won't eat me. Even then I'm trembling like a mouse as she carries me past him. She takes me through the house to play with Dolly in the garden. Every so often that Rottie pokes his head out of the back door and growls. Tamsin says he doesn't mean any harm, but I'm not taking any chances. I leap for Mum's lap and stay there.

I sit and watch Dolly in wonder. That tiny dog has no fear. She runs all over that Rottweiler and even sits on him.

When Dolly first came to them as the tiniest imaginable puppy, Tamsin accidentally left her in a room with the big dog. A few minutes later, when she realized what she had done, she flew back in to find the giant Rottie lying with his enormous bulk spread across the floor, grinning, as if to say, 'Aren't I a good boy? I didn't eat her.'

And based on that, Mum trusts he won't eat me!

21 November

My thick coat has started to come in and I must say I do look rather magnificent. Mum remarks to a friend of hers, 'Venus is beginning to look like a polar bear!' Well, I've seen polar bears on television. They are enormous creatures. Do I really look like a polar bear? Me? I nip to the mirror and sneak a look at myself. I stand on my back legs and even practise a deep 'Grrr'. I will be fabulous when I grow up! I'll be more powerful than a Rottie.

Mum's got a friend coming round today with her Labrador mix. Apparently he eats like a horse, which is a change from me, the fussy princess. But I'm watching with great interest. Is the woman bringing hay for him to eat? Will he eat grass? Is he huge like an elephant? When he arrives he looks just like an ordinary dog and we play together in the garden. Humans are very odd. What does she mean when she says he eats like a horse? I saw him eating dog food! My angel says if people would speak with clarity there would be more understanding in the world – and I totally agree.

Chapter 13

Fun and Play

22 November

As he was a rescue cat, Brutus, the tabby, never learnt to play, so it's obviously my job to teach him. A few weeks ago I used to take my life into my paws when I ran after him. Now that I'm getting so much faster, I can chase him and get away with it. Mind you, he's still twice my size. Now he sometimes stalks me, then chases me, and I love it because I'm quicker than he is. Today I keep a few paces in front of him, my tail waving madly in the wind while he pursues me twice round the lawn. He's gloriously cross.

Brrr. It's cold outside. The wood-burning stove is glowing orange, so it's lovely and cosy in the kitchen. From my basket I notice that Brutus is crossing the room to sit on a rug by Mum's feet. What a cheek! But I'm not called White Lightning for nothing. I make a dash past him and claim the rug first. Then I look at him with innocent eyes. Well, you won't believe what he does. He stalks over with stiff legs to *my* basket and sits in it. Is that a declaration of war or not? I can't believe my eyes. What can I do? I give him a dirty look, which he ignores, and a little while later when he closes his eyes, I nip over and dare to sneak my toy out of my basket. Brave, huh!

My angel points out gently, 'Venus, it takes two to tango!'

Tango! I'm not dancing. I want my basket and my toy and the rug by the fire. I want everything.

My angel doesn't judge, but she does make a note in her special book.

23 November

I wake feeling mischievous and courageous. When I see Brutus sitting on the lawn, I run in circles round him, barking and taunting him. At last he gets so enraged that he chases me round and round the trees in the garden. We really are beginning to relate to each other.

Playing with Mum is different. She throws balls for me, which I run after and pick up, but won't bring back to her. We go over this a few times every single day and she still doesn't get it!

'Bring it, Venus, bring,' she coaxes. I look at her blankly. She comes up to me and puts her hand out for the ball, repeating, 'Give it. Give.' 'No way! I'm a terrier and Papillon mix, not a retriever.'

She wants me to drop it down right by her, especially when she's sitting down and, of course, I know this. She tries, 'Venus, bring here,' and points to the floor beside her, but I'm not stupid. If she's sitting down, I place the ball a few feet away so she has to get up to throw it. I want her to get up and play.

Mum has cottoned on at last that I'm a possessive terrier. So she throws two balls and I gather them up. Next, she runs across the lawn to me and I run from one ball to the other picking them up in turn. Then, at the last moment, I have to make a decision and charge off with one of them. This game is much more fun!

We are in the middle of playing this when Elisabeth comes home. It's ages until Christmas, but already she's buying little presents for her children.

My pink angel murmurs to me that even if her kids are not consciously aware, they will be energetically picking up the love she feels. I do hope so. I can see pink light flowing from her heart when she talks about them.

24 November

I'm not a little fluffy puppy any more, but I still wriggle my whole bottom with enthusiasm when I wag my tail and I do love to bound around and play like a puppy.

Today I earn my bronze badge at puppy training. Mum says it's important so we have been practising the tasks every day. Before we enter the hall Mum asks the angels to enfold me and help me. Phew! That really calms me down as I feel their energy touch me. I don't want to boast, but I do everything absolutely perfectly during the test.

Mum has brought some chicken with her to reward me each time I do something right. That just may have been a mistake, as I'm rather more focused on the treat than on the instructions, but it does mean that when she says, 'Sit!' I'm down in a flash. Chicken!

Mum has to answer all sorts of questions at the end of the test and she's more nervous than I am. But she gets them all right, thank goodness. I would hate to fail because of her. When the dog trainer announces that I have passed, everyone claps and cheers, 'Well done, Venus.' You know what, I see the angels are celebrating, too!

And my friend Buddy the Maltese, passes, too, so we are going up into the silver class together.

My angel tells me that in the golden age of Atlantis people competed without any sense of rivalry for the sheer joy of doing their best and that's what it feels like tonight, we are all cheering each other on.

25 November

Mum has set up a little agility course for me in the garden. A plank is resting on a bench and I run down it, then over a jump and through a double-length tunnel. I love practising this and I like the rewards even better.

Having said that, when I think she isn't looking I run round the course just for fun – but don't tell her!

What's on the bench?

26 November

Mum has added another hurdle to the agility course, without asking me! I feel very put out and the only way to register my disapproval is to sit in front of the extra one and refuse to jump, so that's what I do. Sometimes I even run round it.

Mum hops over it to show me. Does she really think I don't know what she wants me to do?

27 November

I have decided to be magnanimous and accept the extra hurdle. Actually it's quite fun and I get lots of praise.

We also have a little climbing frame in the hall for the small grandchildren and Mum is teaching me to slide down the chute and run through the tunnel. It's very easy but I won't do it unless there's a treat waiting. Mum says there should always be an energy exchange and a biscuit is my payback!

28 November

Elisabeth is still looking for Christmas presents for her children. With the help of Ben's friend's mother, Mary, she has purchased a sweatshirt for Ben and toiletries for Annie. She has expended so much love in buying them that I'm sure they'll be pleased. Perhaps they'll even persuade their dad to let them see her.

My angel reminds me that when you do the right thing with the right intention, the universe supports you, even if it's not in the way you expect.

Chapter 14

Through the Ice

29 November

After days of rain, it's freezing cold today. All the streams have overflowed and the field bordering the forest looks like a lake. The water has something strange and white on top of it, like cold, hard glass – it's ice!

I run through the fence to what was the grassy meadow and for a time enjoy slipping and slithering on this slippery stuff. Mum calls me back and I return as fast as I can, but as I reach the wire fence, the ice cracks under me. I disappear under terrifyingly cold water. Mum screams, 'Venus!' in panic and races towards me. I flounder wildly and try to scrabble onto the hard ice again, but it keeps breaking off under my paws. Somehow I bulldoze my way through it under the wire and onto the path. I shake myself like a dog who's demented, until I'm warm.

Phew! White is obviously dangerous. If it's not swans, it's ice.

Mum's friend is walking with us and has seen what happened, so Mum recounts the story of Justin, her son, going through the ice when he was seven years old. When she tells this story her aura goes grey and shivery and blobby, so I know she's still holding the shock inside her.

She explains that the family were living in Holland at that time and they went skating on a big canal. Suddenly Justin, with all the impetuosity of a seven-year-old boy, charges off on his own, racing as fast as he can. He's heading towards thin ice, head down, oblivious of everything else. Mum chases desperately after him, shouting his name as loudly as she can, but in vain. Sure enough, the ice gives way under him and he goes through. By luck or angelic intervention he spreads out his arms as he falls, so the ice holds him and his head is above the surface. As Mum gets near to him, the ice under her cracks, so she spreadeagles herself and wriggles towards him on her tummy – and manages to grab him. With the superhuman strength that is given to mothers on such occasions, she pulls him out and carries him home.

Mum says that Justin's Guardian Angel has always worked overtime with him, both as a child and as an adult, and deserves a medal. My angels nods vigorously in agreement. 'Did you help me when I fell through the ice just now?' I demand.

'Of course we did,' they say together and add, 'We work as hard to help and protect you as Justin's Guardian Angel does. You have lots to experience.'

'Thank you,' I respond, in a small, happy voice.

Later, sitting quietly by the log burner, I ask Mum telepathically for more information about my Guardian Angels. 'You know all animals have two angels?' I nod. She fetches her laptop and shows me a picture of a cow with two Orbs on it. Orbs are the dots of angel energy that appear on photographs. Then she shows me a glorious photograph of a bright yellow Orb by a dog. I can feel doggy goose bumps. 'That's Archangel Fhelyai, the Angel of Animals,' she tells me. 'He and his angels look after all animals everywhere. He will send one of his beautiful yellow angels to help you, if you ask.'

I chat to Mum

So that's why animals often have a yellow angel with them. That feels warm and comforting.

Mum walks me round the block at dusk and I jump onto the low wall of a neighbouring house. What's that? I nearly fall off backwards with shock. There's a cat with big shining, glittering, green eyes in the front garden, looking as if it's ready to pounce on me.

Mum smiles and says, 'It's alright, Venus. It's not a real cat. It's a metal one with glass eyes.'

Who would play such a trick on an innocent dog? My heart is still pounding. And where was my protective yellow angel?

30 November

When Mum goes out, if she's going to be longer than an hour, she says, 'Shopping, Venus', so I go upstairs and sleep on her bed until she gets back. She usually returns with bags of food and I sniff around them hopefully, for treats. Recently, she has been coming home with mountains of boring stuff and apparently this is due to something impending called Christmas. Why do people have to go out and buy clothes and things?

My angel tells me that Mum and I once lived together in a golden era called Atlantis, when we materialized what we needed and life was so much easier and simpler. Everyone lived contented, honest lives with integrity and joy, always acting for the highest good.

I can't help wondering if people really need all this *stuff*?

1 December

Mum and I fit in a quick visit to Justin and Rachel and two-year-old Maya before Christmas. It's a joy to run around with the gentle little girl again, and she and I have a great time playing together in her Wendy house. I even hide in there and have a nap while she's doing something else.

The other good thing is that I get to nip out into the garden to sniff the chickens. Pity they aren't so happy about it.

2 December

Something terrible happens – absolutely, unbelievably horrid. We all go for a woodland walk with Maya in a pushchair. It's icy cold with a bitter wind. We come across two large pools with a narrow, moss-covered wall in between them. Being an intrepid explorer I trot along the wall. When I notice a grassy embankment below me I jump onto it, *but* it isn't solid. It's like quicksand – an illusion – and I plunge straight through it into freezing, watery sand – and disappear!! Mum screams loudly, 'Venus!' and starts to crawl as quickly as she can along the slippery wall towards where I have vanished. She can't see me. A lady passing calls out unhelpfully, 'Oh, dogs have often done that. It's terribly dangerous. That place is notorious.'

I struggle, choking and covered in thick sand, to the surface and dog-paddle blindly towards Mum. She heaves me up to safety and I shake myself over her. I'm shocked and frozen to the marrow. We all hurry back as quickly as possible in the biting wind.

Mum bathes me in warm water and cuddles me in a hot towel, while I ponder the lesson.

Perhaps it's, 'All that's green isn't grass'. Maybe it's, 'Things aren't always what they seem to be.' On the other hand it could be, 'Take the plunge in good faith and trust the universe will support you.' On further reflection I think it's, 'Sometimes you have to go through difficulties before you are wrapped in a warm, fuzzy blanket.' Yes that's it, I decide as I fall asleep, warm and cosy on Mum's lap.

Chapter 15

Celebrations

3 December

Today is Isabel's 9th birthday, so Mum and I have driven to their house for her birthday party. Kali, the cat, appears to touch noses with me and then quickly disappears again. I don't blame her. I'm sure she knows something is going on! Pretty soon a whole crowd of girls arrive and I bark at them, so Mum picks me up and tells them that they are to leave me alone. That's better. Lots of angels are arriving, too, and I wonder why?

A tall man wearing a strange hat turns up. It transpires he's a magician. All the children sit around him, while Mum, Lauren and I stay at the back and watch in awe. Everyone is clapping, cheering, ooh-ing and aah-ing. How does he do those amazing things? My name is Venus Magic. I wonder if I can be a dog magician?

The angels are still with us and I can see that they are enjoying the party, too. When Isabel's cake is brought out, candles flaming, the angels cheer with us. They are laughing and dancing. They say they always attend weddings, parties, graduations, ceremonies and celebrations of all types. They bring with them the spirits of the loved ones of the participants! Yes, they bring all those grandparents, aunts, uncles, brothers, sisters, cousins and friends who have passed over, so that they can watch and celebrate with joy and pride. If you find yourself thinking about a loved one who has died, it's probably because they are with you.

I celebrate too

5 December

Wallace, the Schnauzer, is very good in crowds and with groups of people. I wish I could be like him. He stays calm and comfortable whatever is going on around him. I'm different – I panic and become very nervous.

My angel tells me it's because I'm so sensitive, and it's true that I feel everyone's energy. She says more and more people are becoming sensitive like this and it's important for them to cleanse and protect their auras, as well as to stay grounded.

Every day Mum takes me for long walks to ground me, calls in Archangel Michael to protect my aura and visualizes a diamond of Archangel Gabriel's light over me to purify my energy fields. My angel says that Mum is doing the right thing and it would help a lot of humans if they did this, too.

Andrew has a huge and eclectic selection of friends and is always willing to support them. That's how I come to be in a large crowd this evening, with Wallace. I feel like a cowering white blob while Wallace looks like a smart, confident, gentleman dog. He's friendly with everyone and lets them stroke him. I don't.

Andrew's friend John, who also comes from South Africa, has cancer that has been progressively getting worse. He has had several rounds of chemotherapy and radiotherapy; now the hospital in the UK has refused him more treatment and sent him home to die. But in South Africa they will give him another round of chemotherapy. He wants to go there, but he is struggling to pay for the treatment as well as his flight and accommodation.

Mum says she doesn't understand how burning and poisoning a person can heal them of cancer. It's a bit like blood-letting in the past. But the power of love can heal.

Andrew obviously believes in community and the power of love. He gathers everyone together and puts on a concert to raise £10,000 to send his friend to South Africa for another round of treatment. And right now I'm at the concert with Wallace, watching love and generosity pour from everyone's hearts.

John is leaving for South Africa tomorrow. He looks very thin and fragile. I do hope all this community love sustains him.

8 December

It's a busy shopping time. The new lodger is always at home, so there's someone in the house to keep me company, but mostly I lie on Mum's bed and wait for her to come back.

15 December

Elisabeth has finished wrapping up her children's Christmas presents. We have lit a special candle for their happiness.

23 December

The house feels really weird. There are shiny baubles dangling everywhere, but I'm not allowed to jump up and grab them. Strange bits of coloured paper are hanging from the ceiling and, most peculiar of all, there's a tree in the hall! A tree, I ask you. That is odd enough, but today Mum has draped coloured lights and sparkly stuff all over it. Apparently, this is a Christmas tree, which is evergreen (or plastic) and symbolizes life and hope in the darkest part of winter.

Mum tells me that the family will be arriving tomorrow. Yes, all the grandchildren – so it will be the usual chaos. I sigh, but I might as well surrender.

My angel smiles at me and reminds me that surrender to the Divine will is a very advanced lesson. Clearly, I'm a very evolved dog if I'm being brought all these lessons! I manage to wag my tail to show I'm ready.

24 December

Elisabeth has texted her husband to tell him she will be leaving presents for the children on his doorstep very early on Christmas morning. Mum looks horrified and says, 'Why have you warned him in advance?' Elisabeth replies that not even her husband will do something slimy at Christmas.

I wouldn't be so sure.

Christmas Eve! Before the onslaught of family, we have a little quiet time and I lie on the sofa. I notice that the energy feels different today, like rainbow silk. My yellow angel looks extra sparkly and joyful, though quite serious. She sits by me and I feel an electric tingle through my body, so I know that she's going to impart some important news. She tells me that we are about to enter an extremely important cosmic period that occurs every year. Apparently a flow of divine energy streams into the world after the winter solstice and it becomes a torrent at midnight on Christmas Eve. Ooh! I can sense it already.

Every year on 25 December people can access special fast-frequency light, carrying higher information and cosmic wisdom. This is why this date is celebrated as a religious festival in many ancient civilizations, and a number of the great masters were said to have been born on this date, though they actually incarnated during a different season. I can't say that I understand all this, but I nod sagely and act as if I'm a very knowledgeable puppy. My angel continues that it's really important to find a little quiet time to absorb the special light, as it can boost animals and people to another spiritual level and enable them to access more Christ light – the golden energy carrying pure unconditional love.

Well, it would be good to find some quiet time, but will that be possible when the family is here?

They've arrived. Oh, my goodness! It's like a space invasion. How could they all get here at the same time, three mixed carloads of adults and children?

Mum thought it might snow early so she bought a few toboggans, and the older kids are willingly emptying the cars and sledging all the cases and bags through the house to the hall, where they're piled in an untidy mountain. I have a good sniff around, but nothing smells interesting to me – in other words, no chicken!

Now Isabel and Finn are pulling the little ones, Kailani and Maya, on sledges in the Metatron room, where the carpet is gloriously thick. That baby, Taliya, tries to get to me. She stretches her arms towards me chanting, 'Dog, dog, dog!' but she can only move slowly, so I have plenty of time to retreat. I have to keep a watchful eye on the others though, as they are all buzzing with excitement. I think I'll vanish upstairs while the going's good.

I'm too late! They want me to sit on the sled. Oh, silly me! When will I learn to withdraw in good time?

It's dark early and suddenly the lights fuse. I heave a sigh of relief and nip upstairs to Mum's bed. Thank goodness there are no children in it! I have an inkling there soon will be, though.

25 December

My first Christmas Day!

Isabel tries to put a red Father Christmas hat with a white bobble on my head. I turn into a wriggly eel and Mum intercedes. Thankfully, she recognizes I'm Venus the Papillon terrier, not a docile lapdog. While they have breakfast I escape upstairs to enjoy some quiet time until someone finds me.

The children are soon busy opening presents and playing with them. They are very happy and I see several angels bringing the spirits of relatives who've passed away to join in the fun. It's much easier to come through the veil between the worlds on a day when the frequency is higher. One, who looks very youthful in her spirit body – I think she's Mum's Irish grandmother – is dancing a jig with the children and having a wonderful time. They can't see her, but they can sense her presence and are all excited.

In the afternoon we go for a walk – a strung-out mob of adults, children and me. When I'm let off the lead I run into the trees and onto quiet paths. There I see an elderly lady pottering along sedately with her equally old poodle friend. All of a sudden a glorious shower of golden light flows over them. It only lasts a second, but I know this is the Christ light my angel was talking about. I look around carefully and see that the trees are being bathed in this beautiful energy, too. They are bright and shimmering. Wow! Christmas really is special. I hope Mum and I get a few minutes to relax and absorb the light.

Bedtime
We do. It happens when we are sitting in bed at the end of the day.

26 December
Today is Boxing Day, so-called because of the old tradition of giving servants money from a wooden box. I think Mum should recognize my loyal service with a dog Boxing Day.

Elisabeth is waiting for her friend Mary to phone. She's desperate to know how her children, Annie and Ben, liked their presents. The call comes at last.

Mary reveals that when she and her son popped in to wish them Happy Christmas, their father was in the kitchen re-wrapping the gifts Elisabeth had so lovingly chosen and left on the doorstep. Not knowing that Mary had been with Elisabeth when they were bought, he held up Ben's sweatshirt. 'I got last-minute extra presents for the kids,' he smirked. He then wrote, 'Love from Dad' on cards and taped them to the gifts.

In front of Mary and her son, he also told them spitefully that their mother didn't even love them enough to remember them at Christmas. Mary says their faces went grey and their eyes became dull. It's heartbreaking.

And so Elisabeth cries and waits. Come on universe, something *must* change soon.

Chapter 16

Elisabeth Sees Her Son

3 January

Elisabeth hurries into the kitchen looking very excited. She tells us she has just seen her son, Ben, in the supermarket so she quickly dodged behind a shelf to watch. It's three years since she left, so he's bigger and taller than when she last saw him. Every bit of her wanted to rush out and hug him, but she knew this would give him a terrible shock as his father has told him that she doesn't live in the UK any more and doesn't care about him. So she drank him in with every fibre of her being and held herself back.

'He doesn't look happy,' she confesses. 'I know he needs me. I'm not so worried about Annie. She's older and to all accounts has a nice boyfriend, so she has some support. Also, she has started university, so she's out of her father's influence and I hear she's happy. But Ben believes everything his father says. He really believes I don't love him.'

Despite this she's grinning all the time and looking so happy to have glimpsed him. Her Guardian Angel is standing very close to her and I bark twice just to say hello.

5 January

Elisabeth is sitting on a bench in the garden stroking Brutus while I'm sniffing round the flowerbeds. Suddenly, for no reason, he bites her hard, drawing blood. She screeches in shock and pain, and then, to my enormous surprise, she grabs him and bites him back. I sit and cheer. Mum is looking out of the window and laughs. Brutus glares and scowls ferociously. At last the worm has turned and Brutus has got his comeuppance. He's mortified and, for the next half hour, sits in the middle of the lawn with his back to her. Elisabeth can't quite believe she did it, but Mum says he had it coming to him.

My angel looks a bit startled because it's so unlike the gentle Elisabeth but he murmurs, 'If you treat any creature with disrespect, there will always be a consequence.'

10 January

Every day this week at school-leaving time Elisabeth has driven to the supermarket in the hope of glimpsing her son again, but she has not seen him and she is looking quite despondent. I sit by her in a gesture of solidarity. Dogs are very sensitive and always know how people feel, so I'm sure I'm helping her just by being here.

12 January

Elisabeth has not been to the supermarket for a couple of days and typically, today, when she least expects it, she bumps into Ben with his friends in town. This time he sees her. Apparently, he goes white, bursts into tears and runs away. Now she feels awful.

I am a sensitive dog

But at least he knows she's around.

I smell change in the air and consult with my angel, who agrees with a smile. She responds. 'When you are on the ocean looking for land, you see birds acting as signs that you are approaching your destination. This is the same for Elisabeth.' I wag my tail in sheer delight and jump up at her to try to impart the news. She doesn't get the message, but she laughs with me.

14 January

Elisabeth's husband has found out that Ben has seen her. He's incandescent with rage and is sending her rude texts and threatening to withdraw the boy from school in the middle of term and move out of the area if she dares to go near him again.

She's trying to progress their divorce but he's stonewalling at every turn. Mum suggests she does another uncording exercise to free herself from his energy. *Good idea*, I think, and I'm keen to watch what happens. Maybe I can even assist. Cats usually assist with spiritual psychic work, so it should be Brutus's job, but I have helped Mum with healings in our past lives together.

They light a candle and Mum helps Elisabeth to put down grounding cords and then invokes Archangel Michael to place his deep-blue cloak of protection right around her. I move position slightly, so that the blue light can use my energy to flow round her as I realize she needs very strong protection. She relaxes comfortably and then invites her husband to sit in front of her. His spirit arrives in an angry rush and we all jump. I see his dark energy move around her throat, trying to strangle and shake her. No wonder she has had a sore throat! She coughs as if she's trying to clear it away. Mum asks her to pull the cords away from her throat, but it's a struggle because, no sooner have they been removed, than more sneak in from another direction. In the end Mum asks Archangel Michael to stand between Elisabeth and her husband so that his energy can't come near her. I see a column of blue light form between them and nod my approval. Then Mum invokes Michael to cut and dissolve the tentacles that are trying to crush Elisabeth energetically.

Elisabeth breathes more freely after that.

Next, they look at her solar plexus. This is where people and animals hold fear. Elisabeth has been so manipulated by that man that her chakra is tight with terror. To me it looks as though he's constantly punching her here to try to subdue her will. Mum calls in Archangel Michael to hold his spirit fists away from Elisabeth. Wow! That's interesting. I actually see Michael's blue light pour round the man's wrists and hold them back. Then she invites Archangel Uriel to fill Elisabeth's solar plexus chakra with golden confidence and a sense of worth.

The woman's colour is coming back and something has definitely been cleared from her aura, but already I can see more dark feelers coming from her husband, trying to get through to her again. It's an exercise that she needs to keep doing if she really wants to shake him off and regain her power. I don't think this is the first lifetime he has controlled her.

To my surprise Brutus strolls across the kitchen and sits on her knee. She's so grateful for this sign of support that tears flow down her cheeks. Typically, no one realizes how much *I've* done to help. Still, I shall be a noble martyr dog, helping the world and bearing the lack of recognition with fortitude.

Then Mum says, 'Thank you, Venus. You were brilliant.'

I wag my tail in acknowledgement and lie down modestly before I fall asleep.

17 January

Something has definitely shifted energetically. A date has been set for the divorce and Elisabeth has applied to see the children, but she gathers from her friend Mary that her husband is still poisoning the children, especially Ben, against her,

21 January

What a blow. Ben has written a letter to the court saying that he doesn't want to see his mother again. Elisabeth knows this is her husband's influence and she must accept it and wait until her son is ready. She's anxious not to upset him more. She still lights a candle every day and visualizes herself with both her estranged offspring. I do admire her patience and hope it pays off.

I look enquiringly at my angel who affirms that when you hold a vision without doubt or deviation, it *must* come to pass. I wish the universe would speed up time.

23 January

Elisabeth has a lump in her stomach and she has postponed going to the doctor for ages, as she has been trying to heal it with visualizations and spiritual work. It has reduced quite a bit in size, but it's sapping her strength and interfering with her work.

25 January

This morning Elisabeth is going to the hospital for a scan.

She comes home white-faced, as the lump is growing outside her stomach wall and she has to have an operation.

26 January

It's one of those days with a moody sky and no sunshine. Mum has gone away for a few days to give some lectures, so the new lodger is looking after me. He takes me for a long walk, thank goodness. Elisabeth has gone into hospital in readiness for her operation tomorrow.

27 January

The new lodger is sending healing to Elisabeth for her operation. He says with conviction that his healing will do the trick. There's blue-green healing energy in his aura but lots of dark colours, too, while his angel is standing patiently beside him trying to touch his heart.

I'm also sending Elisabeth healing and dogs radiate it from the heart with no demands or expectations. Then the angels can use it.

29 January

Elisabeth is home. She's looking very pale but she's smiling and is as independent as ever. A friend of hers is staying at our house to look after her. So many people are sending her prayers for healing that her bedroom is full of blue light and there are hosts of angels with her.

It's lovely, but I want Mum to come home. Tomorrow, they tell me.

31 January

Elisabeth is getting stronger and I like to sit cuddled up with her.

The new lodger takes me to the coach station to meet Mum. I'm so excited that I make little squealing noises and jump all over her and lie on the pavement. I'm just beside myself with joy. I want to lick her to pieces and I can tell she wants to hug me forever.

I'm curled up in bed with Mum. Peace.

2 February

Elisabeth hears from her friend Mary that Ben isn't at school.

Why?

His father wants to move away from the area to be with his girlfriend, who lives in the north. He's insisting Ben goes with him but the boy doesn't want to go. Mary has said Ben can live with them to finish his studies, but his father says he needs his son's social security money to live on and, what's more, his son owes it to him.

Mum and I stare at her, goggle-eyed. You mean such things really happen? People actually say these things?

Yes.

I glance at my angel who whispers. 'The energy is changing and when it's right, things will move very fast.' Wow! Watch this space.

5 February

The story today is that Ben's father has let him go to school, but he still says he's moving north and Ben has to go with him.

Elisabeth is very concerned. She knows what a bully his dad can be and Ben is quiet and sensitive like her. He's not a robust young man who can stand up to his father. He's been browbeaten and cowed, just as she was. He's also been systematically turned against his mother and no longer knows where the truth lies.

7 February

Elisabeth hears that her ex-husband is packing up the house and preparing to do a moonlight flit without paying the rent. Apparently he has done this before.

It's emergency time. Elisabeth's friend, Mary, decides that no matter what, she's telling Ben the truth about his mother. Elisabeth is relieved, yet worried for her son's state of mind.

His dad is planning to flit the day after tomorrow and take Ben by force, if necessary.

8 February

How life can change in one day! Mary has told Ben a huge chunk of the truth. He's shocked, but also relieved.

I ask my angel if Ben is all right and she replies, 'Truth has a resonance and things are starting to fall into place for him.' That sounds good.

Elisabeth goes to Mary's house to meet her son for the first time in years. It's an overwhelming occasion.

9 February

There's a phone call. Ben has left his dad's house and taken refuge at Mary's.

Elisabeth contacts her older son from her first marriage, who's a gentle giant, and he drives for three hours to come and support his brother. They meet in a café and talk for the first time in ages. The father won't try anything against this 6 foot 4 inch young man, who's built like an oak tree. He's staying with us for the night while Ben is at Mary's. I like him, but don't know why Elisabeth called him. I could have defended them all. I'd love to bite Ben's dad (with love and light, of course).

10 February

Elisabeth's older son gets up at the crack of dawn as he has to set out on his three-hour drive back to work. So, we all rise early and Mum takes me out.

We've just come home after a fabulous romp in the forest where I chased a squirrel and two birds, and played with several other small dogs.

Elisabeth comes home from work at about 8 p.m. Apparently her ex has driven off in a loaded car leaving the house empty and she's worried about Ben's two cats. Has the man abandoned them? And what about Ben's stuff?

After a bite to eat she collects Ben and his friend. Then they drive round to the empty house. There's no sign of the cats but there are piles of black bin bags. They search through them by torchlight and retrieve some of Ben's clothes, his school uniform and his books. They take them to Mary's.

I think they are very brave. That horrible man could have been lurking around waiting for them, but Mum says I've watched too many detective dramas. Real life isn't like that, she tells me. And she expects me to believe her after this last week?

11 February

Ben is staying at Mary's for the time being, but she doesn't have room for him long-term and social services are involved.

The boy receives a text from his father this morning. If he wants his iPod, laptop and other stuff back, he must send £400. That is a shock and neither Ben nor Elisabeth has that amount of money. They fear Ben has lost it all. At least the father seems to have taken the cats and they think he will look after them.

Ben is in a complete muddle and doesn't know who or what to believe. He doesn't want to live with his mother, who is a stranger to him after three or four years apart.

Mum says that if he changes his mind, he can, of course, stay with us for a few weeks until they get a house. He can have the guest room as long as he vacates it when we have visitors.

17 February

Social services have found a foster placement for Ben locally. He will move in next week. Elisabeth is both relieved and sad at the same time.

19 February

Ben has changed his mind. After a week of contact with his mother a chink has opened in his mind. He says he wants to live here with her until they get a house. Gulp! A house with a teenager and all his friends. I know life is about experiences, but this is ridiculous. Will I be able to enjoy any beautiful silence in the next few weeks?

22 February

Ben has had a text from his father to say that if he doesn't send £400, he will take the cats to the RSPCA. We all feel sick. Elisabeth contacts the man's girlfriend who seems surprisingly nice and says she will keep them until Ben and Elisabeth move into their own home.

The search is on for a house they can afford that will take cats. Mum says, 'You'll miss Brutus.'

'No way!'

Chapter 17
I'm a Teenager

1 March

The first thing Mum does every morning is to look into my eyes, stroke me and say I'm the most gorgeous puppy in the world. Naturally, I agree with this and squirm with pleasure. I love it.

But today she looks at me and says that I've grown into a stroppy teenager. Huh! Just because I don't come the minute she calls when I'm chasing squirrels and birds… or if I want to roll in something foxy and delicious. What a control freak!

On our morning walk I'm chasing around the meadow and she summons me back. Boring! She calls and calls. When I eventually do run back to her she's cross with me. Why should I go to her to be scolded?

While we are on our afternoon walk, Mum seems to have a change of heart. I'm enjoying myself, dodging in and out of the trees in the forest, but this time when she calls me to her, her voice sounds warm and she opens out her arms and smiles. A beautiful pink light shines out of her heart. Oh wow! I race to her straight away.

She says, 'Oh Venus, it's my fault. You need carrots not sticks.' I must say, she does get things wrong sometimes. I don't like carrots – nasty orange things. But I *love* sticks. I pull them out of the log basket in the kitchen and chew them to bits on the carpet. Mum says it makes a mess! *I* think it decorates the carpet beautifully.

13 March

Buddy, my white Maltese friend, is now a teenager, too, and he won't leave me alone. Mum says his hormones are raging. Luckily, I'm much faster than he is and he can't catch me. That's good now that I'm bigger and want a bit of space, because you know what boys are like.

Buddy is a teenager

22 March

I'm eleven months old now and have what is delicately termed my first 'season'. There are some very annoying consequences, such as I have to be kept on a lead all the time. Mum bought an extending one for me, but it's not the same as being free to chase the squirrels and birds in the forest.

Something dreadful happened this morning. (I absolutely hate water, always have done – it's nasty wet stuff – so I run away as soon as I hear words like 'bath' or 'wash'.) Anyway, in the forest the main paths are lined with wide ditches that fill with water when it rains. They are overflowing right now but I'm such a good jumper that I leap over the ditches and run about on the other side in the trees like a jungle explorer.

It was Mum's fault. She should have made that lead shorter. I take my usual flying leap over the flooded ditch, like a winged dog-angel, forgetting I'm on an extending lead. It lengthens but reaches its limit while I'm in mid-leap. There's a moment of suspended shock, then I drop with a horrible splash into the middle of the water. Mum yells 'Venus!' and frantically pulls the lead while I paddle until I manage to scramble out.

I'm very cross with her, so I shake myself all over her and soak her. Then she has the nerve to say that I smell disgusting and gives me a bath when I get home.

I thought this morning was bad enough but she never learns. We go for our afternoon walk along that same path where the ditches have flooded. Quite naturally, I forget I'm on a lead. I make a heroic, Olympian leap across the water, but once again I reach the limit of the lead and land with a terrible splash in the middle. Luckily, I'm saved – but when will she look after me properly?

Needless to say I have to have another bath.

As I fall asleep I ask my Guardian Angel petulantly, 'Where were you when I was nearly drowning this afternoon?' She replies very lovingly that she had her wings around me to save me. Then she adds that I must take responsibility before I jump into the unknown. Me, take responsibility? What about Mum? Huh!

27 March

I'm supposed to stay on a lead for three weeks while I'm in season. Mum hates to see me restricted, so, as no other dogs are about, she lets me off. I'm so thrilled that I want to find a way to thank her. After a little search I manage to find some fox droppings and roll in them. I know she'll be delighted that I smell of doggy Chanel No 5… but she isn't! I can hardly believe she puts me straight back on the lead again. Such ingratitude.

There's another dispiriting thing about being in season… Well, it's a bit embarrassing really. I thought I'd be really attractive to male dogs and get lots of attention while Mum fights them off, but they scarcely notice me. What's wrong with me? I'm young and beautiful and smell divine. And here's the worst bit, female dogs won't leave me alone – not just with bottom sniffs, which I can understand, but they're even trying to jump on top of me! Mum says this will soon pass. I hope so. I haven't been able to see my friend Buddy because he hasn't been 'done' – whatever that means.

Yet another weird thing is happening while I'm in season. Every time I sit on a chair or a bed, Mum jumps up and spreads a cloth under me. Oh well, I may as well enjoy it while I can.

28 March

Mum's been on that computer all day. I decide to take my toy to her and gaze at her expectantly, until she plays with me.

It works. She grins at me, 'Okay, Venus, you win.' Then she closes down that box she attacks with her fingers, puts on her anorak and we go into the garden together. She gets this funny machine called a scarifier out of the shed. It's to get the moss out of the lawn and it's brilliant fun helping her.

She ties my toy on a long string to this machine and I chase it up and down the garden. That keeps me busy for a while. Next, I have a good time jumping in the great piles of moss that she sweeps up. I scatter it everywhere. She laughs the first time I do that, so I do it again and again to please her.

Then I fetch my tennis balls and keep dropping them just in front of the scarifier, so that she has to stop and throw them.

Someone said I'd got her round my little finger, but that's not true – I have paws, not little fingers.

29 March

I really miss my long walks each day. Well, we do wander around in the forest, but I'm still on a lead because of this season thing and I want to run free.

We visit Tamsin's house and I play with Dolly the Chihuahua for a while. Then Mum takes off her fleece and spreads it on the sofa beside her. I snuggle up to her quietly and she says I'm as good as gold. Gold! What's that? Actually, it should be 'as good as a wolf'. That's a proper compliment.

When it's time to leave she puts her fleece on again and discovers why I was so quiet. I was nibbling a hole in the pocket and have eaten all the treats she left in there. She says, 'Oh Venus, you are a one!' but she's laughing, so I'm not in trouble. What does she expect a bored little dog to do?

It's just like that time she took me to visit an old lady. She kept saying how good I was, lying quietly on the floor at her feet – until she realized I was busily chewing the fringe on the sofa! After that she moved me onto her knee where there was nothing to do but sleep.

The saying shouldn't be 'The devil finds work for idle fingers', rather it should be 'Angels find munchies for bored mouths'!

30 March

Oh my goodness! We've had a call from Andrew to say that his house has burned down. He sounds very shaken. Apparently he took Wallace, his miniature Schnauzer, down to the pub for half an hour. When he returned home neighbours were milling on the pavement, watching as smoke poured out of the windows. He rushed inside and opened a door, only to be hit by a fireball. Everything is destroyed.

Mum shivers. She says she can't bear to think what would have happened if Wallace had been left at home. Then she says, 'Of course he wasn't inside! His angels would have made sure of that. Clearly, it's not his time to pass over. Silly me for even thinking like that.'

Andrew lets us know they are staying with a friend until he can find somewhere to live that will take a dog. He also tells us that they think the cause of the blaze was an electrical fault, possibly a faulty lead to the computer. How dreadful! How life can change in an instant.

4 April

We have lunch with Andrew and he takes us around his incinerated house. I've never seen anything like this charred ruin. Everything is burned to nothing. Wallace's tail is right down, which says it all because he's always exuberant. He explains that it's his home and he's now a territorial dog without a territory.

It's not even my home but Mum says I look like a despondent cur. Well, she would, too, if she was a sensitive dog like me. I'm empathizing with poor Wallace as we go round this blackened shell. I'm not impressed by her comment.

There's one flicker of light in the darkness, reminding us that Spirit is always waiting silently to help.

Andrew tells us that his grandfather died before he was born, but he had an icon of St Ignatius, which was very precious to him, so he left it in his will for his future grandson, who was yet to be conceived. Andrew has always treasured it and it hung on the wall in his office. He sadly assumed it was destroyed along with everything else in the fire, but the firemen discovered that it had fallen behind a metal filing cabinet and was completely untouched. Amazing! I love to hear these stories and Mum does, too.

Chapter 18

Strange Meetings

6 April

It turns out to be another of those strange days. Mum and I are meandering along a path through the woods when we meet a man wearing pyjamas, a dressing gown and slippers, with a flat cap on his head. Mum frowns and says this is most weird and we should find out if he's all right. So she stops him and asks him where he's going. He seems very vague and won't tell her where he lives, so Mum tries to keep him talking.

I sit very quietly by her. I don't bark or anything. At last another man walks towards us down the path and our man in the dressing gown and slippers takes fright and runs away. Mum is very concerned about the man in his nightclothes. She doesn't have her mobile on her, which is typical! She hardly ever carries it. She stops this walker and asks to borrow his mobile to call the police as she feels the man is in need of help. To her surprise he says he isn't phoning the police about something like that, and walks on.

So Mum and I call on the angels and ask them to look after our lost soul. A few seconds later a couple we've never seen before appear. They are very pleasant and, when Mum asks if they have seen the confused man, they are extremely concerned about him.

They offer to walk back in the direction he ran away in the hope of finding him. So Mum says we'll go the opposite way round the loop, and we continue on our way – thank goodness. I had a horrible feeling I might not get my exercise, but I have a great run. We don't see the confused man again and Mum keeps saying she hopes that he's safe and someone is looking after him. When we get home we light a candle and ask the angels to protect him and guide him home. Mum also says that she'd like confirmation that he's safe.

7 April

We'd never seen that nice couple before and blow me if we don't meet them again today! They tell us that after they left us they located the confused man and talked to him for a long time. Eventually, he remembered where he lived and they were able to take him home by car. His wife was out searching for him and was most relieved to see him.

Mum believes the angels brought the nice couple along at the right moment to help that poor lost man. And then when she asked for confirmation that he was safe, the angels sent them back again to tell her. I think so, too. It's wonderful how angels encourage people to do things or go somewhere.

8 April

As I've explained before, it's a dog's duty to dislike the postman. Even though Mum introduced me to ours when I was a tiny puppy, I have never warmed to him. He's squat and tubby, wears shorts with falling-down socks and, worse still, pretends to like me. When I rush out barking, he backs away from me, holding his postbag in front of his bare legs, saying, 'I'm not scared of it. I like dogs.' And all the time the hairs on his legs are standing up with fear.

This morning Mum says to him, 'Perhaps you could give Venus a treat?' But he replies that he isn't allowed to give dogs treats. It's 'against Royal Mail rules'.

9 April

Although it's my duty to dislike postmen, I confess I actually like the thin one that comes today. I dance around him, barking, and he says, 'Hello, Venus. I've got a Jack Russell at home. Can you smell him?' and he holds out his hand for me to sniff. Then he gives me a treat. I still bark a bit because it's expected, but he's not bothered.

Mum says that all people react to energy just as dogs do and I'm sure she's right, but dogs are super-sensitive to the feelings people emanate. You can never fool a dog.

11 April

The chubby postman in shorts has given Mum an official warning from the Royal Mail about dangerous dogs. He says everyone in the area is receiving the notice, but we don't believe him. Is he inferring that I, Venus, fluffy little white Papillon–Jack Russell am a dangerous dog, just because I bark at him?

12 April

Mum has put up a post box outside the house as the chubby postman in shorts said he couldn't deliver to our house any longer because I bark at him. She says it's a real nuisance. She really means I'm a real nuisance but she doesn't want to upset me.

13 April

Today we are on our way home from the woods when a Royal Mail van races past us the wrong way down the one-way street. The driver is a new young postman, who is laughing his head off. Sitting beside him is my chubby enemy, also roaring with the thrill of it. They are shocked to see Mum.

They turn into our road and park the van opposite our house. When we reach them, Mum puts on her most school-marmy voice and says, 'That wasn't a very clever thing to do, was it?' They are both giggling like little girls. The plump postman replies bashfully, 'No, it wasn't.' But they continue to snigger behind their hands, as if it's the most exciting thing they have ever done in their lives.

They hear Mum's tone of voice. I wouldn't do it again, if I were them.

14 April

We see the chubby postman in his van and he waves and grins at us, as if we are his very best, long-lost friends.

15 April

The chubby postman gives me an 'illegal' treat, which I eat – but I still don't like him.

19 April

In the woods I'm scampering along the main gravel path in the plantation, when who do I see but Michael, my big Alsatian friend, with his Greek rescue brother! I'm just about to run to greet them when they see me, and charge in my direction. They are enormous when they are free. It's too much. I turn and race for Mum and hide between her legs. Their owner laughs in a sympathetic way and says, 'Changed your mind now they're off their leads?'

In a word, 'Yes!'

Michael on the prowl

Chapter 19

My First Birthday

22 April

It's my first birthday today and I have chicken for breakfast. Lucky me! I haven't changed my food habits over the months, though. I still carefully remove every single grain of rice and all the vegetables with my nose and leave them in a pile by my bowl before I gobble up the chicken.

Mum says I'm still a fussy princess when it comes to food. I prefer to eat fir cones and bits of wood to the organic, additive-free tins and pouches she gives me. I flatly refuse dried food.

Sometimes the new lodger is a vegan; at others, a vegetarian. But right now he's eating meat. He has cooked himself chicken and I sit hopefully outside the door of his room for much of the day.

My friend Buddy, the Maltese, gives me a card and some dog treats. How thoughtful!

Mum brushes me while my angel strokes my ears and tells me that a birthday is a very special day. It's the anniversary of the moment you choose to incarnate and it affirms that you are very important and beloved by the universe. My pink angel whispers in my ear, 'The angels always sing to you on your birthday.'

'Okay, but do I get an extra treat?'

In the afternoon Mum takes me to the forest, as usual. She stops, as you do, to talk to an elf who is sitting on a low branch, so I manage to roll in the mud while her attention is diverted. Mud, glorious mud! Oozing, sticky, odorous goo! I'm caked in it but she won't give me a bath on my birthday, will she?

Oh Mum, how could you?

Evening

I'm lying in my basket thinking about my first year. I'm less fluffy and even more beautiful. Everyone who walks in the forest knows me and lots of people give me treats and pat me. Life is good.

I'm becoming so grown up. A deer runs out in front of me this afternoon and I start to chase it but come back when Mum calls me. She exclaims, 'Wow! That's progress, Venus.' The truth is I'm feeling a bit tired, but she doesn't know that so I get lots of praise.

28 April

It's very muddy in the woods after all the recent rain and Mum definitely needs her Wellington boots. Luckily she likes splodging in muddy puddles, like Peppa Pig – and with all those granddaughters we know a great deal about Peppa Pig.

We take a shortcut along a wide rutted path that turns out to be inches deep in sludge and brown water. Halfway along it we meet an elderly woman struggling through the thick, sticky mire with a stick in one hand and the lead of a boisterous black retriever puppy in the other. The pup is dragging her and she's slithering and sliding all over the place.

It leaps towards me as puppies do, and I'm sure its owner is going to take a tumble. Mum clearly thinks so, too, and insists on taking the puppy's lead and the owner's arm. At first the lady protests that she can manage, but then she acquiesces and tells us she's recovering from a broken hip and is very grateful.

Talk about an accident waiting to happen! She'd have been pulled over by that young dog sure as chicks come from eggs. Oh dear, that makes me think! Sometimes Mum gives me an egg, but I have never seen a chick come out of one. I'll look very carefully next time. Actually, I don't really know what a chick is, even though Mum often tells me I'm the cleverest dog in the world and that I know everything that's going on.

It's true I know most things.

29 April

Of course! I've just realized a chick is a baby hen.

5 May

On my walk this morning I have a really good time racing along and jumping over the muddy ditches. When we get home Mum says she needs to give me a bath. She says I smell terrible – another false human perception. Sometimes I can't believe what people say.

Mum always says you should be careful what you ask for. I'm being good as gold standing in the warm water in the sink in the utility room, when she declares, 'I wish this shampoo would come out more quickly!' What a silly thing to wish for. The top immediately flies off and shampoo gushes out. In no time I'm up to my ears in copious soap bubbles. I can hardly see through the stuff. I struggle and manage to slip out of her hands and along the work surface. She shouts 'Venus!' as she tries to catch me. I should have been shouting 'Mum!' But she manages to capture me and it takes ages to get all the froth off. Finally, she says I'm 'squeaky clean'. Wrong again. Does she think I'm a mouse? I'm more like 'growling clean'.

10 May

You'll never believe what has happened to me today. Mum announces that I'm going to be spayed, whatever that means. She tells me she's leaving me at the vet's and the angels will look after me.

I'm not concerned because there are always angels in our house and I know they look after me. I'm not even suspicious when she lights a candle and says, 'This candle is for Venus. I invoke Archangel Raphael to give her healing, Michael to protect her and Fhelyai, Angel of Animals, to look after her.'

I saunter into the vet's with my tail wagging, expecting a treat. They make a huge fuss of me and I love it. Then the vet sticks a huge needle in my bottom. Ouch! I squeal very loudly. Mum says she will hold me while I go to sleep. What do they mean, sleep? I'm wide awake. Then a funny thing happens. My eyelids start to blink very slowly, then they droop and a lovely yellow angel, the Angel of Animals, strokes me.

Next thing, I wake up with a woozy feeling. I can hear Mum's voice, so I stagger out to her and she picks me up gently and carries me to the car.

Evening
I lie in my basket and let Mum feed me a little chicken by hand. I notice the candle Mum lit for me this morning is still burning and there's lots of green and blue around me. That means Raphael and Michael are helping me. I sleep again.

11 May

I sleep nearly all day cuddled against Mum in the conservatory. She has her laptop on her knee and says she can't leave me even for a moment in case I jump down by myself. But I don't want to move.

A workman knocks on the door and I don't even have the energy to bark, but I do gather all my strength and crawl to the middle of the kitchen to protect Mum.

She promises I'll feel better in the morning.

12 May

Mum's wrong. I don't feel better.

She shows me my collar and lead and says brightly, 'Walk, Venus!' My ears droop and I groan, 'Oh no. Not a walk!' I bury my head under a blanket.

So she holds my water bowl up for me and feeds me some more chicken by hand. I sleep all day.

13 May

Wow, I feel better today! The back door is open and I race round the garden to claim my territory, just in case any birds or squirrels are taking liberties. Life is wonderful!

I prowl round my territory

I dig a hole in the middle of the lawn and Mum doesn't even tell me off. She says I'm digging to Australia, which is very odd. Doesn't she know I'm digging to find the bones I've buried?

Mum is so pleased to see me looking better. She reminds me about 'As above so below'. If you do something for a friend and they don't bother to say thank you, you feel less inclined to help them next time. She explains that the energies of the universe respond in exactly the same way and we must remember to thank the angels who have looked after me. So, we light a candle and say thank you.

Chapter 20
Summer Madness

1 June

I'm recording this at the end of a long, hot day during which I learn something extraordinary. I'm still shocked by it! Here it is... *Everyone sees things differently!* What about that? When something happens everyone sees it with different eyes. For example, if ten people look at me, they register me in ten diverse ways. It's weird. Nevertheless, I bet no one likes the plump postman, except possibly his mother.

Anyway, this is what happens today. When we get up Mum tells me that I get more gorgeous every day and I'm the most beautiful dog in the world. Now she should know, shouldn't she? But, here's the revelation – not *everyone* thinks so.

This is how I find out. We go to a Dog Day with Kathy and Buddy, my Maltese friend. It's in a big field and there's a colourful array of tents and hundreds of dogs about. Everyone is very friendly and I sniff loads of animals.

There are all sorts of competitions and stalls that sell doggy things. Mum has me measured and – on the hottest day of the year – orders me a coat for the winter! It's violet and I swear

I'll never wear it. My angel smilingly wags her finger at me and suggests I keep my options open, but I wave my tail and remind her I'm a terrier. She pretends to sigh.

Mum puts me in for the Prettiest Bitch competition. It's a bit undignified. I'm expected to trot in a circle by Mum's side while people look at me and pass comments. This really isn't my thing. Then we have to sit. In protest, I make sure I plonk myself on my beautiful tail and let my ears droop so that I look like a miserable mongrel. The judge just walks past me without a glance. I know then that she has no taste – and I turn out to be right. A very ordinary-looking brown-all-over dog wins. It hasn't even got one white ear like mine.

My angel murmurs, 'You know, Venus, it's the beauty in your heart that matters. If you are miserable, that's not attractive. It's your spark and spunk and joy that make you special.'

Now she tells me.

I am the most beautiful dog in the world

It's such a hot day that after the prettiest dog competition we have a picnic under some trees by a stream. There are several robust-looking dogs jumping about in the brook, apparently having a wonderful time, but I don't do water. To my horror Mum picks me up and stands me in it, saying, 'This will cool you down, Venus.' It's up to my tummy and even though it's cool, I put on my most dejected expression. I expect her to lift me out quickly but no, I have to splash to the shore myself. I don't even have the satisfaction of shaking myself all over her because she's still paddling while I flop down on the bank.

To make it worse, Buddy, whose legs are shorter than mine, seems to be enjoying frolicking about in the rivulet.

With the intercession of a treat, I soon forgive Mum and snuggle next to her on the bank. My angel chooses that moment to teach me about the wonders of water. 'Do you know, Venus, that the love energy of the universe is carried everywhere by water?'

'Yeah?' I reply.

'This is important. It's not just the water you can see or drink, like streams and rivers and oceans. It's in the air you breathe and the cells of your body! If you bless water, it rises in frequency to the fifth dimension and raises everyone to the fifth dimension, too.'

Is that why Mum always blesses glasses of water, and showers and baths? I've even seen her putting out her hands and blessing puddles!

'Indeed, she's raising the frequency.'

'That's cool!'

'And anyone can do it,' my angel finishes – she can see my eyes closing as I doze in the sun.

8 June

I catch and kill a squirrel. Ha ha! It has teased me for ages and I jump on it and shake it. Then it goes limp. I'm quite shocked, but so excited and very proud of myself. I carry it in my mouth to Mum. My tail is erect, my eyes shining. She tries to take it from me, but I'm certainly not going to give it up to anyone.

I want to carry it home but won't let Mum put me on a lead because she might try to grab it. To get me away from the road she walks back down the path into the woods again and I follow her, dodging away when she gets near.

I hope Michael, the big Alsatian, comes along. I'd love him to see me now. Venus, the squirrel-catcher.

After twenty minutes I get bored, so I drop the squirrel's body and Mum covers it with some twigs. She asks the angels to take its spirit and we watch it rise up in a column of light.

My yellow angel swoops towards me and looks at me without judgement. 'Archangel Azriel is the angel of birth and death, so one of his angels comes to every human or animal when they die to help them pass over. One of Archangel Fhelyai's angels also helps animals to pass.'

I nod. So that explains about the lights I saw hovering above the squirrel.

She continues. 'Archangel Azriel appears dark because his light is internal, so he doesn't radiate outwards.'

'I see.'

'Archangel Fhelyai's angel was the bright yellow one. The other lights were carrying the spirits of the squirrel's family to meet their loved one and accompany him back to Sirius, where grey squirrels originate from.'

'Wow!' I'm surprised.

My angel adds that when animals are killed on the roads, their spirits are often in shock and linger above their dead bodies. She says that if people see a road kill, it's really helpful if they ask the angels to help the spirit of the animal to pass properly.

Now that I understand more, I feel quite sad about that squirrel, even though I'm part terrier. I don't want to catch one again.

13 June

Isabel and Finn and their mother, Lauren, are staying with us. Today we all go into the forest and build a secret lair in the roots of a fallen tree. We collect long sticks for the roof and sides and cover the whole den in bracken. Yes, I help! The children say they are escaped convicts, whatever that means, and we must all be very quiet. When anyone walks past, they crouch in silence inside the den or hide behind nearby trees because no one must see them. Finn and Isabel keep whispering 'Shhh Venus. Remember we're escaped convicts!'

Naturally I think I had better be the watchdog. Whenever a dog comes past, even the ones I play with every day in the woods, I rush out and bark ferociously. I'm doing an important job and I don't know why the children are cross with me.

Later when Mum is quietly stroking me, she tells me about her friend who bought a crinkle dress. She left it hanging up and her husband thought he would iron it for her. He spent two hours ironing it and, of course, ruined it. He really thought he had done the right thing and didn't understand why she was cross with him.

Mum, what are you talking about? I was being a guard dog. I wasn't ironing anything!

15 June

Kali's kittens are due any day. Lauren is worried that there will be too many and she won't find homes for them all, so the children decide to play a trick on her. They phone the friend who is looking after their cat, and persuade her to phone their mother to tell her that Kali has had five kittens.

It works. Lauren answers her mobile. Then we hear a great screech. '*Five!* She's had *five* kittens! Oh my goodness! Five.' She can hear her friend's children screaming with excitement in the background and thinks they are thrilled about the kittens, not realizing that they are laughing at the trick.

Isabel and Finn are jumping up and down with delight, shouting, 'Kali's had five kittens.'

I jump up and down, too, and join in the excitement by barking enthusiastically.

Lauren groans and laughs at the same time, 'How will I find homes for five kittens?'

Then she sees Mum's face and stops. 'You're having me on. Tell me you're having me on?' And everyone roars with laughter for ages, most of all Lauren, but hers is relief.

The angels enjoyed that little hoax because it was fun and there was no malice in it. They love it when people laugh because it raises everyone's frequency. I wonder if it raises the frequency when I bark?

16 June

The children and their mother go home today. They want to be there when Kali really does have her kittens. Thank goodness Mum has made it very clear that she doesn't want one. I couldn't do with her fussing all over a kitten, let alone – horror of horrors – Stray Monster's grandchild.

Kali Has Her Kittens

18 June

Kali Cuddles has given birth to four kittens on Lauren's bed. The children, Isabel and Finn, watched them being born. Kali looked up at them and purred with pride when each one came out. 'Aaaah!' Mum gushes when she hears this. 'That's lovely!'

'What is it with sentimental people?' I think.

But my angel reminds me that a newborn is still linked to Source and radiates pure Divine essence. So when anyone sees a new baby, in that instant it opens their heart to God.

Now I wish I had been there, too.

21 June

Apparently Kali and the kittens have made their home in a wardrobe in the children's bedroom and Kali is being a very good mother, despite being so young.

24 June

Isabel phones to ask if we want a kitten but Mum cleverly says she would only want a grey one like Ash-ting, the magical talking kitten in her 'Tara' books for children. She's sure Kali could not possibly have a grey one.

30 June

Isabel has sexed the kittens and there are two boys and two girls. 'They are gorgeous,' she argues persuasively, but Mum is adamant. 'We've got homes for the girls, but we still need homes for the boys,' Isabel continues.

'I'd never have a male cat,' responds Mum quickly.

2 July

Mum has gone off on another trip and I'm left with the new lodger. He doesn't give me treats like Mum and he's very strict. He says Mum plays with me too much!

16 July

Mum's back today and I'm overjoyed!

17 July

We receive a Skype call from Isabel. Her eyes are shining and she's grinning from ear to ear. She holds up a tiny ball of grey fluff that looks like a rug rat. She says very excitedly. 'Granny, there's a grey one and we've called it Ash-ting because we knew you'd want it. You do want it, don't you?'

An adorable little bundle of grey fluff, with two big eyes, meows.

Well, what could Mum say? She looks at me and we both sigh. I just hope it's not like Stray Monster or Brutus!

My first glimpse of Ash-ting

Mum sounds as if she's trying to persuade herself. 'You know, Venus, it's very important for a household to have a cat. They help to hold high the frequency of a home.' I lick her to remind her we're in this together.

She goes on, 'Did you know that when the vibration of Golden Atlantis started to decline, the first thing the priests did was to send for more cats to try to raise it again?'

'No, Mum, I didn't.'

'And they keep the home clear of unwanted energies and entities.'

'Mmm.'

My angel adds, 'And cats are independent, enlightened beings from Orion, the planet of enlightenment. They come to teach humans.'

I look at her without blinking.

'Oh, Venus! What have I done?'

18 July

There's a stag in our woods. The news goes round the forest like Chinese whispers that he's in the middle of a newly planted area and so Mum and I naturally gravitate in that direction. I must say he's magnificent, standing very tall and still as if we aren't there.

My angel explains that deer are learning and teaching about trust.

19 July

The stag is still there. This time my angel whispers that the stag is radiating out an energy to help people have trust in the universe.

20 July

He's still in the plantation. Today he's lying down so it's hard to spot him among the newly planted fir trees, but I can smell him. Someone squeals that she can make out his antlers and then everyone can see him.

21 July

The stag's reputation is spreading and lots of people are coming to the forest especially to catch a glimpse of him. Sometimes it looks as if the paparazzi have turned up.

27 July

The stag is still there, surrounded by a little harem now!

28 July

My angel tells us that the message the stag is sending out is changing to one of community togetherness. His presence is inspiring people to connect and talk to each other.

29 July

The buzz around the forest is that the stag has escaped from the local deer farm and they are intending to shoot him. Everyone is up in arms. We have asked Steve, one of the regular dog walkers, to find out.

30 July

Mum has taken delivery of a new car. It's all clean and shiny. I can see she's pleased with it because she runs her hand over it and smiles. She opens the door and says, 'Come on, Venus. Let's drive to the woods and go for a walk. We can see if the stag is still there.' She doesn't even fetch a lead. We just jump in.

We wander along to the stag's usual haunt and to our relief, there he is, safe and sound, with three small brown does.

On the way back to the car a dreadful thing happens – and I don't mean it to. I jump over a muddy ditch and it's wider than I expect. I miss. I have never done that before, but I fall into deep, thick mud, so deep I go right under. When I drag myself out mud is dripping from my ears. Mum screeches. She's cross with me and it isn't my fault. We march straight back to the car. The other dog walkers look at me in horror, especially as they know we have a brand new car. They offer polythene bags, but that's the best anyone can produce. Mum has one small towel in the boot. She wraps me in it and plonks me on the back seat, shouting, 'Don't you dare move.' I hardly dare breathe! We get home without me getting one single speck of mud on the seat. She lifts me out, carries me to the sink and washes me ruthlessly.

Later she gives me a hug and sighs as she says, 'All right, Venus. Material things aren't really significant in life, not even new cars. The only important thing is that you are okay.'

I look at her with bright eyes and fetch my toy so she can play with me.

31 July

Steve has contacted the deer farm. They assure him that the stag will not be shot but captured and returned. No one believes him. There's fierce talk flying about.

1 August

I ask my angel about the stag. 'Will they shoot him?' My angel nods and I'm so shocked that I sit quietly for a while, mulling it over. That doesn't feel right. Then I realize I have asked the wrong question. My angel glows very bright as he responds, 'Yes, they will shoot him with a tranquillizer dart before they take him back to the deer farm.'

'You should always be careful with your question and how you interpret the answer,' the angels tell me. I get up and stretch, so Mum fetches my lead and we set off to say goodbye to our stag.

Chapter 22

Brutus Moves House

2 August

Elisabeth has been house-hunting ferociously and holding her vision of a home for herself, Ben and the cat. It's proving really difficult to find a landlord who will take an animal and she's on every possible estate agent's list. I don't imagine they are so keen on teenagers either! In fact, I've got quite used to that *thump-thump-thump* sound coming from the lad's bedroom. Mum says it's called music and 'that's teenagers for you'. Ben offers to take me for a walk tonight, but I don't know him well enough for that, so I flatly refuse to move. Mum exhorts me, 'Go on, Venus. Don't be a silly girl. He'll take you for a lovely walk.'

'No way! You can't be too careful these days.'

3 August

It's the school holidays and we are deluged with family. Ben is very sensibly staying over at his friend's for the weekend, which is just as well because in our house there are bodies sleeping everywhere. Unfortunately, baby Taliya can now move. Whenever she sees me she crawls as fast as she can towards me, cawing her favourite word, 'Dog, dog, dog.' Usually I can slip away, but sometimes I find myself in a corner. I'm not allowed to bark or growl, so I roll my eyes desperately at Mum and so far she's always rescued me in time.

I have to note here that Taliya has a sweet energy and lots of pink flowing from her heart, but she has a huge disadvantage – she's a child.

5 August

They have all left except Isabel, who is staying for a week. I like that. She doesn't really count as a child. Ben is in his old room. Life is back to normal again. But what is normal? Things change all the time.

My angel often declares that your days are only the same if you repeat the same thoughts. If you want your existence to change, send out different pictures to the universe.

I nod vigorously in agreement. I'm always dreaming of chasing squirrels and deer and fantasizing about all the wonderful smells in the forest, and I get all of those things in my life. Perhaps I'll imagine Mum spending all day taking me for walks in the woods. Wow! That would make my life even better. I'll start thinking about that now.

6 August

It's working! Mum says we are going for an all-day ramble. What joy! I am a Master Creator. I can make the life I want.

Later

I've run for hours. I missed my afternoon snooze. My pads are sore and I'm too tired to eat my tea. Perhaps I'll just think about chasing squirrels in our local forest, but I can't even do that. All I want to do is sleep.

7 August

Today we are taking Isabel to a horse-riding lesson. Mum says I can come and watch, too, because I'm good with horses. The bottom line is that I'm good with horses because Mum makes me sit down whenever she sees one and gives me a treat.

We arrive at the stables and I gulp. This is not like the forest where one or two riders walk sedately along the path. Here there are horses everywhere! There's an overwhelming smell of horses and I don't feel very confident, so I stay close to Mum. Once Isabel is on her horse, Mum and I go to the indoor school and sit on benches to watch.

Other mums and grans have brought their pooches, so we go through the canine greeting routine and then I lie down and relax, letting the divine odours pour over me in waves. This is probably the equivalent of a dog spa day. Afterwards, I feel rested and refreshed.

My angel often advises that you should take time for rest and refreshment so that new things can flow into your life. I wonder what exciting new things will come to me now?

8 August

Mum, Isabel and I are going to a big local show today. We don't really know much about it except that there will be lots of animals there and we've heard it will be fun.

We park in a huge field full of vehicles and pray we'll find the car again. Personally, I don't hold out much hope, what with

Mum's sense of direction and the sheer size of the place, but I'm sure the angels will help.

It's amazing here. We hear some creatures that look like small horses making the most peculiar noise I have ever heard. 'They must be ill,' I cry out to Mum in alarm. 'Call the vet. They've got terrible coughs!' But she explains that they are donkeys and that's the normal sound they make. Well I never!

There are dozens of horses, too, but they are in fenced-off areas and we are heading for the dog section.

We find the dog area at last and – guess what – my puppy-class teacher is judging. She likes pugs and bulldogs, so I don't stand much chance in the Mixed Breed Prettiest Bitch Class, but Isabel insists on taking me into it.

Amazing! I get a rosette and come second! Mum and Isabel are delighted.

I love the agility course for beginners. I have to jump over a stick, and run along a tunnel then over a hay bale, through a curtain and round poles. Easy peasy. It's fun the first and second times – well, even the third, fourth and fifth times. But I'm getting a bit cheesed off by the sixth and seventh go. It's worth it though, as Isabel and I are joint winners and she thinks I'm the best pet ever!

By the time we go back to the car, I'm so tired that I let Isabel carry me all the way. Please don't take me for a walk tonight. Having fun can be exhausting.

9 August

There are still no prospective houses coming up for Elisabeth, Ben and Brutus. We'll have Ash-ting the kitten in a few weeks.

Oops! I hope Brutus doesn't eat him. Grrr – not with me keeping watch, he won't.

I hope Brutus doesn't eat him

Mum and Elisabeth energize the projected house move with a ceremony. I sit right inside the circle of crystals.

11 August

Elisabeth has found a house with a garden for Brutus and it's away from the main road. She's absolutely delighted and will be moving there in a couple of weeks. Everyone is looking out pieces of furniture for her. The world is full of kind and generous people, and Mum says Elisabeth has attracted good things by being wise and open-hearted.

I wonder how Brutus attracted a nice house? Does he have hidden depths of wisdom I haven't plumbed? Is he secretly an old soul teaching us lessons? I don't think so, but he must have done something good to have Elisabeth as his owner.

I expect he'll miss me like crazy. Perhaps he came to us so that I could teach him about love? That feels much more like it.

15 August

The house feels quite empty without Elisabeth and Brutus – and Ben, of course – though, being a teenager, he was usually either out or in his room and I didn't see much of him.

Now that I'm a teenager, I like to lie in, too. I don't want to spring out of bed in the early morning like a puppy any more. I sensibly wait under the duvet to see if Mum is going to do her e-mails or have a shower before I get up. She calls me lazy! How could she? This morning when someone comes to the door, instead of charging downstairs, I lie in bed and bark, which in my view is appropriate conservation of energy. Doesn't she realize that I'm undergoing a natural hormonal change? Mum asks if I'm ill, but I just turn on my back and allow her to rub my tummy in the way of a mature sixteen-month-old dog.

16 August

I suppose the new lodger has never really fitted in and Mum is always trying to make excuses for him. But his big plus-point is that he loves me and I often sit with him when Mum is out. I expect the angels brought him here, so that I can heal him.

18 August

Well, there's evidently a house-moving energy in the air. We are visiting Andrew, who has moved back into his house – it has been magnificently restored and expanded. He has had two big bedrooms and bathrooms built into the basement section.

My angel informs us that the pain at times of destruction and hardship causes people to go through an initiation to a higher level of consciousness. Well, Andrew has certainly used this seeming disaster as an opportunity to expand his house, and his aura has expanded, too, and become softer, with more gold in it. So, I guess that's right.

The funny thing is that Wallace the dog's aura is also different. It seems bigger and brighter, like his master's. My angel reminds me that dogs support their owners through challenging times and so they grow spiritually, too. I want to evolve, but I don't want Mum to have too many difficulties to face.

25 August

Mum and I are going to visit Elisabeth and Brutus in their new home. I'm unaccountably pleased that I will see Brutus again.

We find their lovely house easily and Brutus is in the sitting room. I'm delighted. My tail wagging, I rush up to him calling, 'Hello Brutus, it's me. I'm here.'

He responds. 'Oh no, not you again!' and turns his back on me. I'm stunned! Then he stalks out of the door.

I'm a bit subdued after that but Elisabeth gives me lots of strokes and pats.

My angel smiles and pours warm light over me. 'You should never let someone else's attitude affect your mood, because it says more about them than you,' she murmurs lovingly.

She's right. I wag my tail. I'm a super-loved, spiritual, angel dog and I will soon have Ash-ting, my kitten, to look after.

Chapter 23

Ash-ting, the Little Grey Kitten

26 August

I'm so excited, I hardly know what to do with myself! We're going to collect our new little grey kitten called Ash-ting!

It's a long drive and by the time we arrive I'm glad to stretch my legs, so I run in to say hello to my old friend, Kali Cuddles. Mum has warned me that, as a mother cat, she might be protective of Ash-ting, who's the only kitten not yet re-homed. Not a bit of it. She's fed up with him and wants some peace. So Kali and I touch noses and I tell her we'll look after Ash-ting. She's clearly grateful and extremely relieved. Without further ado she wanders off into the garden to enjoy her freedom.

Now for the big moment! Mum holds me while Isabel brings Ash-ting into the sitting room. Whoa! He's unbelievably tiny. I want to run to him and lick him all over, but Mum says, 'Gently, Venus. He's only small.' Yeah, I can see that.

I'm incredibly good. I sit at one end of the sofa and he's at the far end. I thump my tail wildly while I let him get used to me, but I don't move. It takes time but he comes slowly closer.

He meows a baby meow and I can't help myself. I whine with excitement. And by the evening he's happy to sit on the sofa beside me. I feel so protective of him. My new kitten!

I get close to Ash-ting

Lauren, Isabel and Finn repeatedly tell Mum that if she changes her mind they would love to keep Ash-ting. Finn, especially, doesn't want to let him go. I look at Mum anxiously and remind her why we need a cat, but most of all I remind her that he's ours. He belongs to our family now. He's mine.

I don't spend all weekend getting to know Ash-ting. Finn and I play football, which, as I've mentioned before, is one of the most frightening things a dog can do, but I endeavour to be brave. Mostly, he kicks the ball and I try to dodge out of the way.

Also I have a good time sniffing round the guinea pigs' cage. It's a shame they are such nervous creatures. The angels remind me that they come from Venus, which is directly connected to South America, the continent of the heart, and that is why the guinea pigs originally incarnated there. Oh angels, sometimes you are full of useless information! I just want to play with them.

27 August

Ash-ting is in his travel cage on the back seat beside me and he meows all the way home. Yes, he keeps the racket up for an hour and a half. I feel sorry for him, but it's a real relief when we finally stop the car.

After staying awake during the entire journey, he's now asleep in *my* basket in the kitchen. Really, I don't mind. I'm glad he feels safe there and I lie on the floor nearby to guard him.

At bedtime Mum decides he's so tiny that he'll have to sleep in our bedroom where she can keep an eye on him. What sort of insanity is that?

28 August

Rather to my surprise, Ash-ting sleeps all night.

I'm pussy-footing around him – well, puppy-footing really – but Mum says I'm too bouncy and I keep knocking him over. I don't mean to, but he's so very small.

He seems to be settling in. This afternoon Mum asks me to play with him, so I fetch my favourite toy and drop it in front of him. He puts out a paw to touch it, then sits on the floor and licks himself. Boring! I hope he can do better than that when he's bigger.

29 August

I've gone off that kitten. He's a cheeky blighter. You won't believe what he has done!

I've always been particular about my food. I relish freshly cooked breast of chicken and even gourmet garlic sausage. I'll eat cat food, of course, but that's because I'm not supposed to.

Well, Ash-ting is given special kitten food and Mum puts his dish high up, so I can't get to it. My bowl is on the kitchen floor. Today she mixes lots of fresh chicken with my breakfast and I'm starving, so I rush to eat it. To my horror, that little grey furry kitten insinuates himself right under me. His head peeps out from under my chin and he's eating from my bowl with me. The cheek of it! I don't know what to do. I try to push him away with my nose, but he just tucks himself in more securely and carries on gobbling *my* chicken. I glance desperately at Mum, who smiles fatuously and does precisely zero, so I put my head down and eat as fast as I can. Is this the shape of my future? Not even my own bowl of food?

Life is not fair. The kitten's plate is high up and when I climb onto the kitchen table to try to reach it, I'm told off. Yet he's allowed to eat from mine! What's right about that? To make it worse Mum says unsympathetically, 'You're so fussy. Let's see what a bit of competition will do!'

30 August

The honeymoon period is definitely over. At four o'clock this morning I'm fast asleep next to Mum under the duvet. But that kitten is awake. He climbs onto her hip and divebombs me. I wriggle to get away from him but he runs round in a circle, scrambles onto Mum, then leaps onto me again – and he keeps doing it. He thinks it's great fun. He wakes Mum, of course, so she puts him on the floor. A fat lot of use that is! He manages to claw his way back onto the bed and jumps on top of me once more. In the end Mum tucks him firmly under the duvet on the other side of her, so we can all get some sleep.

Later

It's late afternoon and I come racing in to tell Mum that Ash-ting is stuck up a tree at the end of the garden. She runs downstairs with me and across the lawn. There he is on a high branch, meowing plaintively. There's no way we, or even a ladder, can reach him.

Mum affirms aloud three times. 'Ash-ting is on the ground in a perfect way. Angels, thank you for helping with this.'

We stand quietly for a few moments waiting for help or inspiration to arrive. Ash-ting even stops wailing for a moment. And then the new lodger comes home early, climbs the tree by pulling himself up with remarkable strength, tucks the whingeing animal into his jacket, and climbs down again.

Thank you, universe! We asked and you delivered. Ash-ting wanders off ungratefully.

31 August

Mum has gone to Paris and she has asked me to look after the kitten, along with the new lodger, of course. That's a big responsibility for a little dog. All goes well at first and he cuddles up to me and purrs, which is rather nice. I think he's missing Mum. But then, oh no! We are snuggled together in the kitchen and he starts to suckle my teats! I'm paralyzed with horror. I manage to roll my eyes at the new lodger and luckily he sees what's happening and lifts him away.

1 September

Ash-ting is trying to suckle from me again. Help! Come back, Mum!

2 September

That kitten has no respect. He jumps on top of me even if I'm in my basket. He plays with all my toys and eats my food if I'm not quick. I know he's only a baby, but this is ridiculous.

3 September

Mum gets back from Paris and I throw myself at her, I'm so excited and pleased to see her. I keep whining and crying, 'Mum, it's lovely to have you back.'

I call, 'Ash-ting, Ash-ting, Mum's home. Come on! She's back, come and say hello. Can't you see she's here?' And you know what? That kitten walks into the centre of the kitchen and sits with his back to her. And even more astonishing, instead of being upset or cross, Mum laughs and says, 'That's cats for you, Venus.' And she gives me an extra hug. Oh, I'll never understand this world.

Mum and I cuddle on the sofa and she says, 'Dogs are dogs and they have their own characteristics and special ways.'

'Yes, of course. I'm faithful and loving and protective and companionable and wonderful and…'

'Yes, you are all of those things and more, Venus.' She tickles my tummy. 'And cats are cats!'

'I suppose so,' I agree grudgingly. 'Ash-ting is playful and fun and adventurous and he adores me.'

'There you are!'

I can see a twinkle of yellow and my angel adds, 'It's like the various races and cultures. They're all different and when you honour and respect each other's customs and ways without expecting them to be like you, the world will be at peace.'

Just then Ash-ting jumps onto the sofa, snuggles up close to me and purrs. Mum's right. He's different, but I can't help loving him.

Ash-ting snuggles up to me

I don't know why I've never mentioned it before, but every night and every morning Mum lights a candle and asks Archangel Michael to surround herself, Ash-ting, me and everyone in the family, in his dark-blue, protective light. When she does this, bright blue light flashes around us all. Then she asks Archangel Fhelyai, the Angel of Animals, to place one of his angels with me, and one with Ash-ting. She pictures his yellow light around us, then around every animal in the world. After that she tunes into the great Animal Portal of Yellowstone and calls on the light emanating from there to touch all creatures and to help humans everywhere to understand them. I have to confess, it's very comforting. When she has gone through that list she asks the unicorns to pour their pure white light of illumination and higher enlightenment onto herself and me. Whooh! A lovely white shower falls down over us. I wish everyone in the world would do it.

At bedtime the kitten and I play games all over the bedroom, chasing each other round the floor and even up and over the bed, while Mum reads her book and then meditates. Usually she takes Ash-ting downstairs after this. But tonight she just turns out the light, leaving him playing. I quickly dive under the duvet. To my astonishment the kitten plunges in after me. I expect there will be trouble, but to my amazement we all sleep until the morning! Perhaps he's growing up…

4 September

…or perhaps not.

Chapter 24
Life Changes

5 September

Ash-ting is grey and Mum doesn't seem to be able to see him in the garden after dusk – but I always know where he is. This evening, Mum goes outside, searching for him and calling his name. Then she does what she should have done in the first place – she turns to me and says, 'Find Ash-ting for me, Venus.' I run straight to him. I really don't know how she would manage without me.

6 September

I feel that Mum is favouring Ash-ting over me. He gets away with all sorts of things and it isn't fair. She says, 'Remember that Ash-ting is only a baby.' Grrr! Babies are a nuisance! Then she makes a big fuss of me and says, 'I love you, Venus. You're my best girl.'

See, I'm the best one. I run across the hall and knock the kitten over just to show I'm boss and – guess what – Mum tells me off.

7 September

That pesky kitten keeps trying to get out of the garden, yet he's much too small to go wandering like that. I'm doing my best to keep an eye on him but he disappears in a flash. He nearly succeeds this afternoon but, when he reaches the side gate that leads to the road, I lift him by the scruff of the neck and carry him back to Mum. He meows loudly, complaining that I'm being a control freak. Oh, it's such a responsibility to look after a baby.

8 September

I'm finding looking after this kitten more stressful each day. Tonight, after dark, he clambers through the hedge into the garden next door. He's perfectly happy playing on their lawn, quite oblivious to the dangers that I, as an older dog, know about. Mum can't find him and he doesn't come when she calls, so as usual I have to show her where he is. She can see him through a hole in the hedge and tries to lure him back with chicken, but it doesn't work so she has to go round to the neighbour's house and collect him.

9 September

It's impossible to keep that kitten in. He's as thin and slippery as a piece of seaweed. Tonight he's missing again after dark, so I'm sent out to search for him. I find him in one of the big laurel bushes between our garden and next door's. He's right at the top and Mum climbs up with a torch in one hand. But that baby pest is having fun and just wants to play, so he jumps onto another branch.

Mum calls on Archangel Fhelyai, Angel of Animals, to look after Ash-ting, while she dashes inside to open a tin of tuna. She puts some on a plate and runs out with it – but while she's balancing on a branch, holding the plate and torch in one hand and trying to grab the kitten with the other, the fish slips off onto the ground. Lucky me! Mum fetches more tuna and this time she puts the plate on the ground, holding me off it! In a jiffy Ash-ting jumps down and starts to gobble it up. Mum picks him up quickly and carries him inside, while he wails in protest.

My pesky kitten, Ash-ting

10 September

That kitten never learns. This time he goes over the fence to the garden on the other side, where they have a sausage dog. It barks menacingly. I woof frantically to inform Mum that Ash-ting is in trouble, but she tells me to be quiet. That canine next door carries on yapping and when I try to get Mum to understand, she sends me indoors.

A few minutes later Mum asks me where Ash-ting is. Immediately, I run out of the back door to the fence, and whine.

This time she realizes that something is wrong and rushes over. That mutt next door has Ash-ting backed up in a corner! It's a tense moment while Mum scrambles over and grabs him. I receive lots of well-deserved praise this time but that grey fur ball is quite unabashed.

It's definitely unfair. Ash-ting and I are having a fun time tumbling about and jumping on each other. He claws my nose and I let out a loud yelp. Mum shouts, 'Venus, stop it. Leave Ash-ting alone, you bully.' There's no justice. That kitten hurt me!

Even my angel is unhelpful. She smiles, 'Sometimes you just have to rise above it.'

11 September

My life has changed. It's fun to play with Ash-ting, but when I want to play with Mum, he's hanging round, too.

This afternoon I fetch my toy with its string attached so that Mum can swing it for me to catch, but that kitten is racing behind me chasing the string. Mum jokes, 'He'll soon be coming for walks with us!' No! I hope not.

12 September

I'm a very responsible dog. Tonight I go out into the garden to do my business. It's a very dark night and I'm ready to come in when Mum calls me. However, she doesn't realize that the kitten slipped out when she opened the door for me. He's like a mouse – you don't see him slither out of the tiniest crack. So when she calls me, instead of coming straight in, I run to the end of the garden to fetch him. 'Venus,' she calls. 'I told you to come here.'

Luckily, when I reach Ash-ting he comes immediately and we run indoors side by side. Thankfully, Mum realizes what happened and is very pleased. She apologizes for being cross and gives me a treat.

I look at one of my angels, who reminds me that when you do something for the highest good, you eventually receive karmic recognition.

I prefer recognition *now*.

13 September

We are filming a DVD today. Lots of people arrive to take part, but Mum shuts me in the kitchen. Huh! I'm meant to join in. I bark and bark until they let me out. Then I run into the filming room and drink someone's water, which makes everyone laugh. That's my first good deed.

I chase around among the audience and they try to pat me and call me to them, which lightens up everything. Mum says I put her off.

I do other helpful things, too. Every time Mum stands up, I jump onto her chair to keep it warm for her. And when someone lies on the floor for a demonstration, I immediately stretch out above his head, in perfect alignment with him.

My angel reminds me that I did that in the healing temples of Atlantis. We bring our latent gifts into this life with us and they are coming forward now for everyone.

15 September

Mum has bought me some horrible tins of dog food. She purchased them to give me variety and because someone said her pet absolutely adores this brand. Well, that dog is not me! I refuse to eat it for as long as I can and even Ash-ting, who is the greediest cat in the world and eats all my food whenever possible, won't touch it. I think that makes Mum decide.

At teatime she gives me a little tiny bit of this food and mixes it with a lot of roast chicken and a dusting of cheese, so I eat it.

16 September

Mum has to work in London this weekend and there's no one to look after Ash-ting and me, so she's driving us to her daughter Lauren's today to settle us in. Isabel and Finn can't wait to see me, of course!

Everyone wants to know how Ash-ting and his mother Kali will react to each other. Will they recognize each other after six weeks? How will Kali be with her son?

As soon as Ash-ting leaps out of his travel cage on his long, wobbly legs he runs to his mother – but she's having none of him. I watch goggle-eyed as she hisses at him and bats him away. It breaks my heart.

Ash-ting spends the whole time trying to cuddle up to or play with his birth mother, but she doesn't want to know. He jumps playfully out at her whenever she passes. Then he trots behind her, mewing. It's sad to see, except that he's such a cheerful, engaging chap that he soon wanders off and finds something to play with before trying again.

And what about me? I've been his mother for the last six weeks and suddenly he's not interested in me. I'm devastated because I've looked after him for so long. At least every time he really wants comfort, he snuggles up to me and purrs. Then he's my baby again.

My angel envelops me in her wings and murmurs that motherhood is about the heart, not genetics.

17 September

Today is a repeat of yesterday. Kali feels that she has done her duty and she turns her back on her kitten. He really is ours now.

One good thing comes of this. Everyone is so busy watching the cats that I get to sniff around the guinea pig run for a while.

Then we all walk to the station to see Mum onto the train. I don't want her to go and my tail droops, but she smiles and waves before she's swallowed up. They'll never get me into one of those huge great hissing, panting serpents.

19 September

Mum is coming back from London. Ash-ting and I hear her walking up the drive, so we both race to greet her. She picks me up first!

I sleep cuddled up to Mum on the sofa and Ash-ting is nestled up to me.

20 September

Mum and I walk to school with the children. As you know, this isn't my favourite place because of all those kids wanting to stroke me and touch me. Maybe I'm maturing because it doesn't seem quite so bad today. I only bark once at a child who comes too close to me. I scare him off, all right.

Then Mum and Ash-ting and I drive back home. I'm not looking forward to the journey after last time when the kitten mewed all the way, but I lie against his cage where he can touch me and he sleeps the whole way.

22 September

I have always hated the trampoline. Sometimes the grandchildren try to lift me onto it with them, but I escape as quickly as I can. Imagine my surprise when I find Ash-ting up there, bouncing around, having a wonderful time. Naturally I have to try it. I jump up on the stool that has been left out, chase Ash-ting round it once or twice, then realize how exhilarating it is. So he and I race around it while Mum watches us and laughs. Then she thinks she'll bounce with us, too. Whew! Now that *is* terrifying!

27 September

This evening I start my gold dog class – note, it's not puppy class any more. I'm feeling really good about it – that is, until we reach the car park where Mum explains that Sky, my collie friend, will be there but all the other dogs will be new. She says she's sure I'll make friends with them, but I feel a bit nervous.

Sky and her mum are in their car and we wait for them to get out. It turns out that Sky's mum was explaining to her that she'll only know me and all the other dogs will be new. We go in together and now that I'm with Sky, I feel great. We're going to big dog class. We strut round the corner of the building together and stop and stare. The other dogs are enormous – an Alsatian, a golden retriever, a huge red setter and a wheaten terrier stand in a row staring at us, the newbies. Sky and I look at each other and sit down like small children.

But I have to say it's a fabulous class. Those big dogs are amazing. Sky and I watch with wide eyes and try to copy them. What a learning experience!

I do bully the kitten a bit when I get home. It's good to feel like the senior one again.

Chapter 25
The Bicycle Ride

1 October

Isabel will be ten in December. She has come to stay for a few days and I'm looking forward to that, as she plays with me all the time and gives me lots of treats. I love her, even though she sometimes calls me Eeny Veeny. Would you believe it?

Mum has only ridden a bike twice in the last 30 years, which is a bit worrying. She has bought Isabel a second-hand one for the holiday and cleaned hers up. In the forest I often see people on bikes with their dogs running alongside them, and it looks fun. I'm about to find out what it's really like. Today we are venturing on our first cycle ride. Mum insists that she's in charge and should hold my lead. Isabel says she's more experienced and a better rider, so she should have that honour. Age wins so Isabel rides ahead while Mum wobbles along with me.

All is fine for the first 30 metres until we reach the next road, the quiet one-way street that cars hardly ever use. Isabel crosses first and I'm keen to keep up with her, but the only car of the day comes along at that moment. I tug hard to reach Isabel and my collar slips off over my head. Mum squeals and scoots across in front of the car, drops her bike in the road and hares after me. Isabel throws hers down, too, and races to catch me. A new game – Chase in the Road. My favourite! The lady car driver is very patient. She turns off her engine and settles in for a long wait. That's Dorset for you.

After some time I let them catch me and put my collar and lead on again. This time there's no argument – Isabel holds my lead. The lady in the car and Mum and Isabel all wave to each other and I wave my tail.

And you know what, it's fabulous running through the woods with the bikes. We stop and talk to every single dog owner we meet and Isabel tells them all that she's getting a puppy for her birthday.

3 October

Mum goes to the shop and buys a bicycle basket. That's interesting until she actually expects me to sit in it. She must be mad! There's no way I'm going to get into a basket on the floor, let alone on a bike. I hear her say that she'll look for a bigger one on the internet, one that has a proper dog harness. With a bit of luck she'll forget that idea. She will probably ask the angels to find her a dog basket if it's for the highest good – and I can tell her it isn't.

Isabel has already started a campaign to get a puppy for her tenth birthday. Her mother definitely doesn't want one, but Mum says that Isabel is a master manifester. Watch this space!

This is what she has done so far.

She tells absolutely everyone that she's getting a puppy for her tenth birthday.

She talks about it all the time as if she already has one.

She has cut out pictures of dogs and pinned them on her bedroom wall.

She visits the charity shop or the pound shop weekly and buys something for the dog.

She has promised her mother that when (not if) she gets her pet, she will do jobs to pay for its food.

Every day she asks the angels to bring her a puppy if it's for the highest good.

I'm agog! It's two months until Isabel's birthday. She's going home today and I'll miss her.

8 October

We are walking around the outer edge of the forest when a big black retriever races along the path and up to Mum. It's really strange. This animal is acting as if he really knows her. But he's nice to me, too, and lets me sniff him. Soon two women arrive on the scene and one exclaims. 'Wow, he really loves you!' The other one says to Mum, 'You're the lady who rescued me from the mud after my hip operation!' The big black retriever is rubbing his head against Mum's leg. I can't believe he remembers after all this time.

We chat for a while and when we move on Mum says, 'That's why dogs are so special – they remember.'

Isabel phones to say she has bought a dog bowl in a charity shop.

10 October

Isabel phones to say she has bought a dog collar in the pound shop.

13 October

Humans do say strange things. Mum says her eyes have gone square staring at the computer screen. But I keep looking at her and her eyes seem exactly the same as usual to me.

In the afternoon Isabel phones to say one of their neighbours has given her a rubber bone for the dog.

16 October

Isabel phones to ask if she can have my cage for her puppy. Mum says it's somewhere in the garage and she's welcome to it.

19 October

The weather has turned. It's pouring with rain – thick, grey, relentless rain. 'Oh, lovely', cries Mum cheerfully, all warm and dry in Wellington boots, mac and umbrella. She actually hums to herself as she splodges through puddles, while I'm like a drowned rat – miserable is hardly the word for it. Water is dripping off my ears and tail. I refuse to run and play in the trees. Instead, I plod behind Mum like an old lady. Every so often I paw feebly at her leg to implore her to take me home. 'Won't she ever get it?' She announces, 'Okay, we'll walk down the little paths under the trees. It's not so wet there.' At least that's better, but when we reach the main path again, a curtain of water hits us. At last she relents and heads for home.

When we reach the road I streak as fast as I can towards shelter. Finally, we arrive at our house, where she has the grace to wrap me in a warm towel and rub me dry, then snuggle me into a soft rug and settle me down on the sofa.

Is this love?

20 October

I'm not on speaking terms with Mum and she thinks I'm a terrible teenager just because I don't want to share with Dolly the Chihuahua when she comes to play today. Usually, we share our toys and chews and play together all the time. But she's *my mum* and they are *my* chews and I also have to explain that Dolly and Ash-ting played together and left me out. So when *my mum* gives us all a salami stick treat, I wolf mine, grab Ash-ting's right out of his mouth and go for Dolly's. I'm like lightning.

Later, Mum gives Dolly and me a chewing strip. Normally, we play tug-of-war with them and it's a great game, but I seize Dolly's and place it carefully between my paws while I eat my own. I growl at Dolly every time she tries to retrieve it, so she sits on the sofa and watches mournfully.

Mum is very unkind. She takes my strip away! How mean can anyone be? But I'll show her. When she takes me for a walk in the woods I refuse to go to her when she calls me. She immediately turns and heads for home and I can't find her for ages. When I do see her, I race to her and she puts me on my lead. I can't chase birds or squirrels or jump ditches. Huh! See if I care.

In the evening I refuse to sit on her chair beside her. I cuddle with Ash-ting on another chair. He loves me whatever I do.

21 October

During our morning walk we meet a couple with their Jack Russell. A puggle puppy has followed them and they tell us that its owner is at the other end of the woods. Mum says she'll take the puppy with us as we are walking that way, but it refuses to come. In the end Mum puts him on my lead and offers him a treat. That does it. All the jealous terrier in me comes out. My *lead!* I growl menacingly and dart in to grab the treat before he can eat it. Every time Mum tries to give that imposter on my lead a biscuit, I snarl and snatch it first.

I'm not an unreasonable dog. When she explains that we are taking the puppy to find its owner, I settle down. That's all right then, but she should have told me sooner.

The puggle pup and I race along the path together, ahead of Mum. He's touchingly pleased to find his owner and she's so relieved to see him again that she shouts at him for running off. I can't think what I was jealous about.

At bedtime Mum strokes me and whispers, 'Venus, you know you are special and I love you.'

'Of course I do.'

'Then why were you jealous of that little puggle?'

I close my eyes and pretend I'm asleep because this conversation doesn't make me feel good. Mum is not fooled. 'Jealousy means you are afraid of something. What are you afraid of?'

At last I say in a small voice, 'You might love him more than me.'

'Open your eyes, Venus,' she says in a soft way and I feel safe enough to look into hers. At this minute I can only see love, and I feel warm and loved and secure. But I know that this good feeling will fade away and the old insecurity will come up again. Mum seems to realize this. She puts her hand on my chest and says, 'Now Venus, I'm going to ask Archangel Chamuel, the angel of love, to touch your heart and fill it with such love that the old jealousy dissolves.' Wow! I see a beautiful pink light and feel a warm glow in my heart centre. Suddenly, I love everyone and everyone loves me.

Mum hugs me. 'We may need to do that lots of times and then you will feel happier and safer.'

22 October

I still feel warm and loving this morning. It's beautiful in the forest. The sun is a soft yellow ball in a vast blue sky. All is well in my world.

We meet a lady who walks with four collies. Four, I ask you! And they are all big and bouncy. To keep them engaged she throws a ball and they all chase after it.

Well, Mum is strolling along, enjoying the autumn sunshine and, unusually, I'm right behind her. The collie owner sees us coming, so she lines up the dogs and tells them to sit until we have passed before she lobs the ball. The only thing is, she waits for Mum to pass, then throws it and I get flattened in the stampede. Not funny. 'Oh sorry!' she says nonchalantly to Mum. 'I waited for you, but I forgot about the dog!' Have you heard anything like it? I need a lot of comfort, I can tell you.

Chapter 26

Lessons on Being Lost

23 October

Sometimes Mum hides from me. She thinks she's clever, but I always know exactly where she is. This morning she lies on the floor at the end of the bed. Of course, I know she's there! I creep across the duvet, then peep down over the edge so just my nose, ears and eyes are visible and look questioningly at her. I put on my 'what are you doing there, silly Mum?' expression. She laughs and says, 'There's no fooling you, is there Venus?'

She says I'm a laugh a minute. I hope that is a compliment. She often says that angels love laughter because it lightens everything up. My angel winks at me. I could have told her that.

24 October

Today we are walking in different woods with a friend of Mum's. Oh wow! I'm enjoying the unusual smells in this place. Unlike our forest the trees here are deciduous and it feels very light and airy despite the thick undergrowth. I follow Mum and her friend closely for a while, until I'm seduced by the magic of this fresh world. They are so busy talking that they don't bother to wait for me. In fact, they have forgotten all about me as they stroll along the interlinking paths.

Suddenly, I look round and there's no sign of them. Oh! It's scary in the middle of a strange wood. I run down all the paths we have taken and many we haven't, but my people have vanished. The sun is going down and it's starting to get dark. I will admit I'm panicking. 'Stop, Venus,' I say to myself. 'What would Mum do?' Of course, she would ask the angels to help me find my way. I do this and relax. Then I remember God's gift to me – my voice. I start barking.

All at once I hear Mum's voice shouting, 'Venus! Venus!' over and over again. It's a long way away. I rush towards the sound. Please, please carry on calling me. And then I'm on a wider path and Mum is standing there holding her arms out for me. I race as fast as I possibly can towards her.

She picks me up and swings me round and says, 'We've been searching for you, too. I asked the angels to help me find you and here you are.' It's getting rapidly darker and I walk so close to Mum I'm almost a Velcro dog. From now on I will always keep an eye on her.

25 October

On our walks today I have been Mum's shadow. She says it feels very peculiar, as I'm usually a streak of white lightning in the distance.

26 October

I know all the paths in our local forest like the back of my paw. I could run around them blindfold, so I can never get lost here.

Also, I'm rather clever. I sprint away from Mum through the trees and have a great time for ages, then I return to the place where I calculate she will be. I'm always spot-on accurate. But I do so this morning and she isn't there. I realize she has taken a different route from usual without telling me, so I sit watching in both directions, waiting for her to appear. And I wait and wait. Where are you, Mum?

After a while I see her hurrying down the path towards me. Someone apparently told her I was by the glade. I run to her in relief, but it's a bit worrying. I wish she'd just walk where I expect her to and then this would never happen.

27 October

This morning Mum loses me *again* in the woods. I think the universe is teaching me a lesson about something, but I'm not sure what it is.

She says it's my job to watch where she is! That's rubbish. I like to be a free agent and roam where the action is. I say it's *her* job to stick to the usual paths so that I can find her easily.

She says we would soon be bored and it's more interesting to try a different route each day.

Well, I agree with that as long as she doesn't lose me. I point out to her telepathically that she was with some other people and they were all deep in conversation, which is why she didn't wait for me.

Aha! I've got it. My lesson is not to let her talk to other people in the woods. She should always walk on her own. Then she would be fully focused on me! Now I've understood the lesson, I can relax.

28 October

I can hardly believe it – Mum has lost me again! I find a squirrel and have a whale of a time chasing it round and round a tree. Then I bolt to the car park where Mum and I usually meet. She's not there! I run to the glade that we often wander through. No sign of her! I run back along the track. No Mum!

It's a good job everyone knows me in our forest. I recognize a man who gives me treats, so I stay with him and that feels better. He pats me and says, 'It's okay, Venus. She'll be coming in a minute. She's down there.' He points. That's enough for me. I'm off. I race my heart out – and there she is with a friend. How am I supposed to know she has met someone and has stopped further along the track to talk to her?

I'm very pleased to see her, but she's getting to be rather a nuisance, losing me like this. What can my lesson be?

Evening

We visit Elisabeth and I humbly ask Brutus, the tabby, for advice. He says disparagingly, 'It's a well-known fact that dogs have to look after their masters. You can't expect a human to look after you when they can hardly look after themselves! Just look what a mess they've made of the world! Thank goodness I'm a cat and totally independent.'

I look at Mum anxiously. Is it true that she can't look after herself? I must stand strong in my dog-hood and take care of her.

29 October

This morning I stick to Mum like glue. She says, 'What's the matter with you, Venus? Off you go and enjoy yourself.'

I realize she's just trying to express her independence. Brutus is right. I'm the master.

31 October

It's a truly beautiful morning and we are rambling together down a leafy path. I'm in charge. My tail is erect and I feel big and strong. I vow I will stay close to Mum and ensure she's all right.

A Staffie–Alsatian cross runs towards us and I maintain my ground to protect Mum. He charges straight at me with a growl. What am I supposed to do? At the last moment I nip behind Mum with my tail between my legs. She shouts at the dog, 'Leave Venus alone, you brute.' And pushes the animal away. Its owner calls it off and Mum says, 'It's okay, Venus. You did the sensible thing.'

She protected me! I feel rather inadequate. What is this lesson?

Mum is sitting on the sofa in the conservatory stroking me gently. 'Venus, we need to look after each other. As long as we do that everything will be all right.'

Of course! I lick her hand.

30 October

We walk with Buddy and Kathy on the sandy heath. It's fabulous – lots of new smells. We are meandering through a clump of trees when a rabbit suddenly jumps out! Whoa! I'm after it in a flash and rather to my surprise, I catch it. It utters such a terrible squeal of anguish that I drop it and it runs for its life. The chase is on! Mum and Kathy call me and try to cut me off, but I'm a terrier and I never give up.

The rabbit

I grab that rabbit again and it pretends to be dead, just lying there immobile, so I let it go and dance around it while Mum tries to get hold of me. At one point she calls out, 'Treat, Venus!' and rustles the goodie bag. She must be mad! Does she really think bribery is going to deflect me from my quest?

Suddenly the animal rises from the dead and runs straight towards Kathy, who is standing with her legs a few inches apart. The creature forces its way through the gap. Kathy drops everything and screams and screams! I've never heard such a noise. It echoes and reverberates everywhere and I expect rescuers to come rushing from all directions but nothing happens, except that Mum, Buddy and I are traumatized. In fairness, so is Kathy. I suppose it's a bit unnerving to have a furry rabbit squeeze through your legs – and it turns out she thought it was going to bite her. Anyway, in all the noise and confusion Mum catches me and the rabbit runs off.

I'm rather puffed up with importance but Buddy isn't in the least bit impressed.

2 November

You wait years for something, then two turn up at once. We are walking together in a quiet part of the forest, when I sniff out a rabbit. Wowee! I race after it like a tornado jet, but I think it must be sick because I catch it so easily. It's all soft and grey and furry like the kitten, and I hope it will play but it lollops away. I jog beside it as I do with Ash-ting when we have a race, but this rabbit doesn't seem to think that it's fun.

Just like the other one it flops down as if it's dead and doesn't move. This must be a rabbit sport. Brilliant! It's playing after all. I blank out the sound of Mum's frantic voice calling me, and gently mouth the rabbit all over. I do that with the kitten, who thinks it's a game, but unexpectedly this rabbit squeals blue murder. So I sit by it and lick its ears to pacify it and show it that I don't mean it any harm. Then Mum grabs me and drags me away.

My angel reminds me that it's bad karma to hurt or harm any living creature. That's not fair! I was playing.

Chapter 27
Karma

3 November

The family is staying, as well as an extra child who is determined to chase me. It feels very dangerous and I shiver, ready to growl.

My angel prompts me that fear attracts danger and the best way to be safe is to be harmless. If you are totally at peace and hold goodwill towards everyone and everything, you can't attract any harm. She iterates that not even a bullet can touch you in a war zone. I point out that it's like a war zone here with children everywhere and unfortunately I don't feel calm or harmless. In fact I'm terrified. Mum sees that I'm scared. She picks me up and cuddles me, then tells me she'll keep me safe but I have to relax and trust her. Thank you Mum. I wish you'd done that before.

I lie on the sofa and affirm, I'm always calm and centred, until I fall asleep for half an hour. Then I wake and realize I'm bored. Why is no one playing with me? I jump up and join in the fray.

4 November

Today the sky is light blue and the sun is a pale, watery lemon colour. As it's such a lovely day, everyone is out walking their dogs. I have just run the gauntlet of several big dogs whose owners are chatting on a corner. I might add that Mum is often one of those conversing, but today she's in a hurry. We are walking quickly down the main path when a big dog charges towards me. Its owner is running after it, shouting its name. There's a bad energy around it and Mum obviously thinks so, too. That big dog is coming for me. He's nearly on me. Mum jumps in front of it and tries to grab its collar. This slows the aggressive beast down for a moment, but it shakes her off, dodges around her and jumps onto me, snarling and growling. I squeal as if I'm in the throes of death. Luckily the owner reaches us and pulls it off before it bites me. I'm not hurt and Mum picks me up quickly and hurries away.

Afterwards she says she was in such shock that she could only think of getting me to safety and can't even remember what the dog or his owner is like. Grrr. *I* certainly remember. It was like a gruffalo, only bigger, with yellow eyes and purple prickles and a wart on the end of its nose.

In the evening when I'm dozing on the sofa, my angel talks to me about karma again. 'Venus, everything you do comes back to you: your aggression and anger but also the love and good energy you send out. So it really is worth being gentle.'

I'm indignant. I didn't kill that silly, not-wanting-to-play, probably sick rabbit.

'It's a good job you didn't or that dog would undoubtedly have hurt you more.'

'Oh.'

5 November

Apparently, years ago, a chap called Guy Fawkes tried to burn down the Houses of Parliament in London on 5 November and this event has been celebrated ever since. It's a reminder every year of what many people would like to do. Personally, I think the country should be ruled by dogs and then things would be much better. Everyone would be expected to take long walks in the fields and forests every day and be more connected with nature. People would sniff each other when they met and talked to each other. There would be no postmen. Puppies would take humans to training classes and teach them what to do. Life for everyone would be grand. I'll hold that vision.

Anyway, I digress. Humans in the UK had this dreadful idea of lighting bonfires and setting off fireworks on 5 November to remind us of that abortive attempt. Mum doesn't usually bother to participate but she does this year because the family is staying for the weekend.

We all build a big bonfire. Mum says I'm unhelpful because I pinch twigs from the pile and run off with them, my tail like a flag. Then she chases me so we have a great game around the lawn while everyone cheers me! They're all definitely on my side.

They set out wooden planks on bricks for benches. Then we sit down and everything goes quiet as Finn lights the bonfire. The salamanders, who are the fire elementals, play calmly but happily in the flickering flames and I snuggle between Mum and Isabel watching them.

My angel responds telepathically to my thought. 'Yes, the salamanders are beautiful. Like all elementals they react to the energy of humans. If individuals or, worse still, crowds of people get very excited, the salamanders pick up the emotion and that's when fires get out of control.'

'Is that why candles flicker?' I want to know.

'Well, if the candle is in a draught, the air and fire elementals stir each other up. Or if an angel comes close to a flame that is burning steadily, perhaps to pass a message to someone, the salamanders get very excited and suddenly the flame will flicker!'

'I see.'

'But salamanders love to help people, so you can ask them to get a fire going or to damp it down.'

I'm not sure what else she was going to tell me because I'm fast asleep. It's very quiet and peaceful until an adult says words that wake me up and are etched on my heart, 'Let's light the rockets.'

'A rocket! What's that?'

Mum tries to persuade me to go inside with the small grandchildren, but I want to stay with her and I can be very determined when I want to be. So I sit there, waiting with interest to find out what a rocket is. An adult lights this stick thing and suddenly there's this tremendous whooshing noise, which nearly drives me insane, then coloured lights cascade down from the sky on top of us and, finally, a bomb goes off.

I go berserk and Mum tries to catch me. At last she manages to force me indoors, where the babies are crying because of all the noise. That was really very scary and I refuse to have anything to do with Mum after she did that to me. I lie in my basket and tremble. Thankfully, my best friend Ash-ting climbs onto me, spreads himself right over me and cuddles me until at last I relax. I will never call him a pesky kitten again.

I forgive Mum eventually and she says she's very sorry, that's the last time she will ever have loud fireworks in the garden.

Ash-ting protects me

Archangel Fhelyai says that his angels can enfold and calm animals if humans ask them to. I wish Mum had thought of asking him to help me instead of being so busy with the grandchildren.

Apparently, Guardian Angels and Archangel Michael's angels are working overtime on bonfire night trying to keep people safe, but they can only give limited assistance because humans have free will. Naturally this means that people are free to do silly or dangerous things, so their angels have to stand back and let them get on with it. But if parents ask Archangel Michael to protect their children, his angels will do everything they are spiritually allowed to, to keep them safe.

And the same applies to us dogs. Every morning and night Mum asks Archangel Michael to look after me and Ash-ting. He's probably saved us lots of times.

Chapter 28

Ash-ting the Wanderer

7 November

For nearly a week I haven't had a proper run in the woods because of visitors and rain. Mum says to me. 'Today we can have a really nice long walk. Just you and me, Venus.' I wag my tail and we set off in high spirits.

We cross the road and have almost reached the forest when we hear, 'Meow, meow, here I am!' And a little grey fur ball, looking very pleased with himself with his tail high in the air, is running along the pavement beside us. Ash-ting has followed us almost all the way to the woods. He dances around us and won't be caught. Mum says it isn't fair on me to miss my exercise again, so we enter the forest despite him. Immediately, several dogs appear and a panic-stricken Ash-ting dashes to Mum to be picked up.

Mum calls out to the dog owners, 'I've got a kitten here.' And there's a mad scramble as they try to catch their animals to put them on their leads. Mum pauses, deciding what to do for the best.

At that moment we hear a woodpecker tapping loud and clear on a tree. Now all birds bring messages from the angels and woodpeckers knock to get your attention. We know at once that this message is, 'Get back home,' so we turn round immediately. Well, that kitten struggles and Mum simply can't hold him any longer, so he jumps to the ground. At least he runs all the way back with us. So that's my walk for the morning. And Ash-ting is all puffed up, thinking he's so clever. Not even a 'Sorry'.

8 November

It happens again this morning – that blasted kitten follows us. We are halfway to the woods when we hear the cheery, 'Prrr, here I am.' Mum and I return home immediately and he follows us, but he refuses to come to us or to go into the house. I think *There goes my walk again.* But Mum says, 'Oh Ash-ting, you pest! I don't see why Venus should miss out again because of you.' And we set off for a second time.

For a little while we think he has stayed in the garden, but sure enough, when we're almost at the forest, 'Prrr prrr. Here I am.' And that pesky kitten is with us again, looking as delighted as anything, his tail in the air like a meerkat. Mum ignores him and he follows us into the trees. As we wander down the path, he does look a bit scared, especially when a dog comes along. Then he disappears into the bushes and Mum says, 'It's too bad. Let's leave him, Venus.' We march on for our hour and a quarter around the forest without him and I have to confess we forget all about him.

We're nearly home when Mum says, 'Oh Venus, we've forgotten Ash-ting!' We both secretly hope that he will be sitting on the gate waiting for us, but no! Oh dear! Mum has to get on with some urgent work, but I have a nasty feeling in my stomach that he's lost.

By lunchtime it's been two hours since we left him, so Mum puts me on my lead and we hurry back to where we last saw him. There's no sign of him. We are carrying pieces of cooked chicken and he always appears from nowhere for those, but not this time. She calls and calls without response. In the end she takes off my lead and says, 'Go on, Venus. Go and find Ash-ting.' I rush into the bushes and with my super sense of smell, I soon find that silly kitten hiding up a tree.

I say, 'You naughty kitten. Come back at once.' He jumps down and rubs himself against me, then we run back together to Mum, who is very relieved to see him. Ash-ting must have been scared because he leaps into her arms and lets her carry him back to the gravel roadway.

Once there he knows where he is, so he jumps down and runs in front of us all the way home. After some food he curls up next to me on the sofa and goes to sleep.

9 November

I feel in my bones it's going to be one of those days. It's raw and cold with big drops of relentless rain falling. Mum and I set off for our walk and reach the end of the road to find Ash-ting, that naughty kitten, waiting us. He refuses to go back, so we turn round and go home. Needless to say that stubborn animal won't be persuaded or bribed to go into the kitchen. *Oh dear*, I think, *we've been here before.* Eventually we set off again, ignoring him as he pads beside us.

There's no one in the woods. Everyone else is sitting by a nice warm radiator. We paddle through puddles at the edge of the forest until Ash-ting sees a dog, so he jumps for safety into the hedge of a bungalow. I try to bring him out. I even run round into their back garden but Ash-ting won't come.

It's so cold and wet that we scuttle quickly to the end of the path before we return to the bungalow where we last saw him. There's no Ash-ting, not a squeak or a meow! Once more I run into the back garden but he's not there. Eventually we trudge, soaking wet, back home.

A couple of hours later the rain is more like a waterfall. No sensible creature would go out in it. Mum takes the car to the bungalow and we trudge up and down the path getting drowned. She keeps saying to me, 'Find Ash-ting,' but Ash-ting isn't around. She just needs me as a search dog.

Mum says, 'I bet he's sitting in someone's house being fed sardines.' Grrr. Rain is running off my tail. Anyway Mum knocks on a couple of doors and leaves her phone number, but no one has seen a little grey cat. We trek home again.

At five o'clock, just before dark, we go on another Ash-ting quest. This time we don't drive, but we slog along on foot, looking everywhere, calling his name and knocking on lots of doors. No Ash-ting.

At 8 o'clock Mum decides to search one final time. She lights a candle and asks Archangel Fhelyai to help us find him. It's pitch black, raw, cold and pouring with rain. 'Come on, Venus,' she coaxes. 'We're going for a little walk to find Ash-ting.' Oh no! Not again.

This time, when we are in the deep dark woods, after calling and calling, we hear a cry, a little cat cry and Ash-ting comes charging towards us. Mum scoops him up and carries him home. I'm very relieved, too, but no one says, 'Well done, Venus,' after all the times I've been out to look for him. Ash-ting rushes in and eats my food, then snuggles up to me on the sofa. Everyone says he wouldn't come home if it wasn't for me, he loves me so much. I just wish he'd be a bit more appreciative, but I suppose that's little brothers for you.

11 November

It's only forty-eight hours since the last disappearing debacle with Ash-ting. Today that pesky kitten slips like a shadow behind us when we go out, and disappears somewhere along the next street. When will he ever learn? Is he hiding in a hedge? Oh, where has he gone? Yet again it's cold and raining.

The morning passes and there's no sign of him. Mum and I retrace our footsteps, calling him, but I can tell he isn't there. I have a feeling that this time it's different.

My beautiful angel tells us he's been taken into someone's house. Now what do we do? The new lodger adores Ash-ting and says he'll go and knock on everyone's door around where we last saw him. Sure enough, half an hour later he returns with our naughty kitten tucked under his arm. Apparently Ash-ting sat on the doorstep of this house and meowed until they let him in. He was happily sitting by the fire when the new lodger collected him and was quite reluctant to be taken out into the cold.

I'm glad to have my brother home

Chapter 29
Golden Girl

12 November

Oh dear. Mum's got her suitcase out again. I know she's not going away for more than three days because it's her little case that she calls 'hand luggage', but I'm sitting by the garage door hoping that she'll take me with her.

That's typical, she leaves from the back door, calling, 'Cheerio, Venus. Be a good girl. I won't be very long.' And she's gone. When I was a puppy I used to think she would never come home. Now I'm a big dog I'm philosophical about her trips, but I can't help thinking if she really loved me she wouldn't leave me.

15 November

Mum's home and I'm so pleased to see her. Even Ash-ting has gone up to her and purred, which is unusual for him. Perhaps he's hungry.

She doesn't even have time to unpack before we go out for our dog-training class. It's my gold exam tonight so I'm feeling very special and important. I hate the exercise where I'm supposed to run towards Mum from the back of the hall, then she shouts from a distance, 'Stop! Down!' and I have to lie down between two lines at her command. Usually, I race up to Mum and prostrate myself just in front of her, actually on the line. She's tried all sorts of things to get me to stop between them. What she doesn't realize is that I'm just showing my independence. I'm not stupid. I know what I'm supposed to do. Tonight when it comes to the test, I know it's important for her that I do it right, so when she calls me I move slowly towards her and go down exactly between the lines in the perfect position. I give an exemplary performance and everybody claps and cheers. I do feel justifiably proud of myself, I have to say.

Sky, my collie friend, does it perfectly every time in the lessons. She even lies down immediately if her owner is hiding behind a curtain and calling out instructions from there. That's freaky, in my opinion. Sky thinks so, too, and her eyes roll when she hears the disembodied voice! But tonight, poor thing, she, who always does it right in class, is so keen to do well that she stops too quickly and has to redo that part of the test at the end.

I, on the other hand, am excellent in all the tests tonight. I'm afraid Mum might let me down by getting one of the questions wrong when they examine her, but she has mugged it up on the plane coming home and thankfully gets her answers right. I'm proud of her.

Then comes the big shock. The trainers say that so many dogs have passed their silver grade and are coming into gold that there's no room in the class and we can't continue to platinum level. If a place comes available they'll let us know. I do hope it does.

16 November

Mum has booked me into agility lessons on a farm in the country to take the place of puppy class. The lady running it has impressed upon Mum that it's not just for fun! Apparently, it's 'competition agility' and must be taken seriously. That sounds rather forbidding, but I expect we'll enjoy it anyway. Buddy, my Maltese friend, who is smaller than I am, is coming to the class after ours so we'll be able to compare notes.

17 November

The agility course starts today and Mum and I are really looking forward to it, though it's a shame we decided to go to the early class without Buddy. But I'm sure I'll make other new friends there.

It's a very misty morning and we arrive early. Our instructions are to enter via the farm gate and pass the barns. The track is deep in sludge, so Mum decides to reverse back while it's still possible. One thing you don't know about her is that she can't reverse – has never been able to, apparently. Once she lived in a hotel for six months and drove in a circle around it backwards every single day. The mind boggles, because she still can't reverse for toffee. Perhaps she could for a bone?

Anyway, by the time we have inched and shuffled back and forth and finally parked at the farm entrance, we need to de-stress and a foggy, soggy field probably isn't the best place.

We slog along the muddy track, then down towards the boggy field where the agility is taking place. A woman with a very loud, hard voice shouts at us to go back at once to the top of the hill and wait. Mum and I look at each other and trudge back up to the path and wait… and wait, in the chilly fog. The other dogs in our class arrive… and we wait some more.

We wait

When we finally get to the field the woman with the loud voice lectures us. It's cold and boring. We can't seem to do anything right. We stand around for ages for each dog to have a turn at jumping over a very low pole and we aren't even allowed to play with each other.

I'm fed up with this and don't pay attention. The witch shouts at me, then without warning picks me up. I nip her and she swears! I see Mum hiding a secret smile. How else is a little dog to tell someone to leave them alone? After that the teacher makes Mum pick me up and hand me to her. I give her little warning growls and I have a funny feeling she doesn't like me.

But I promise you I do what she says. I even go through this very long, dark tunnel at her command but as soon as I get to the far end I do a runner through the wire fence, across a meadow to the river bank and sniff around the rabbit holes. What a relief!

I can hear the woman shouting at Mum, 'Go and get your dog. Don't just stand there. Be proactive.' Mum knows that if she follows me I'll run away, so she walks very slowly to the field gate, which is in the opposite direction. By the time she's reached it I've come back to her. I just needed a bit of time out.

Buddy and Kathy are in the next class and don't fare much better, so none of us is going again. But my angel states the universe has a way of working things out for you, so I expect something good will happen to take its place.

18 November

Mum looks at the clock and remarks, 'It's 11:11 a.m. and that is a vibration indicating it's time to move forward at a level higher.'

'Really?' I yawn. This is not really dog stuff.

At that moment our teacher from the dog-training class phones to say there's room for me and Sky and Buddy in the Platinum Class! Hooray. One door closes and another one opens.

Chapter 30
Wallace is Kidnapped

19 November

Where is Archangel Michael now? Andrew has just phoned with some terrible news. It's more dreadful than dreadful – Wallace has been kidnapped.

What! How can that be?

Apparently, while Andrew was talking to someone at the door, Wallace was sniffing about on the pavement as he always does. He's very trustworthy on the road. A car stopped and Wallace was quickly lured into it with a biscuit. Then it roared off.

I'm in bits when I think about it, so I can't imagine what Andrew feels like. And what is Wallace going through? What's happened to him?

Why would anyone want to steal a cheerful little Schnauzer, someone's pet? Mum says there are wicked people with closed hearts, who steal dogs and sell them on for money. They also do worse things to them and she can't bear to tell me about them.

Andrew says there's very little chance of getting him back and the police simply aren't interested. Why not? It's like taking someone's baby. I bet if it was one of the Queen's corgis the police would be interested.

Mum lights a candle immediately for his safe return and asks the angels to look after him.

20 November

Those kidnappers haven't bargained with Andrew. The whole community is looking for Wallace. They are putting up posters, going to pubs and letting it be known that there's a reward for his safe return. Hundreds of people are praying for him and we are sure that Archangel Fhelyai, the Angel of Animals, is on the case.

Mum and I can hardly think of anything else.

21 November

No news of Wallace.

One friend has dared to go to a travellers' camp to tell them about the reward and ask for help in getting him returned. There are some very brave souls in this world.

22 November

Wallace's kidnapping is covered in the local press, so I hope there will be some leads.

23 November

No news of Wallace, but calls of support are flooding in.

24 November

No news of Wallace.

25 November

Still no news of Wallace.

26 November 26

Nearly a week now and hope is beginning to dwindle, but the candle flame is still strong.

27 November

There's been a call demanding a ransom, which Andrew has agreed to. I bark for joy.

In the evening a semi-conscious Wallace is handed over in a car park. He has lost masses of weight and is dehydrated. He has been tied up for a week and his feet are badly burned from standing in his own urine.

Andrew has photographs of the evil kidnappers and their silver Mercedes including the number plates, but the police say they can't take action. What sort of world do we live in? Apparently we dogs are merely chattels who belong to our owners. I suppose it's not so long ago that women were chattels possessed by their fathers or husbands. They fought for their freedom and maybe we should, too. Perhaps I will be like Mrs Pankhurst, a dog suffragette, tied to the railings of the Houses of Parliament. I can picture myself barking against dognappers and puppy farms and animal cruelty.

Mum and I light a candle to thank Archangel Fhelyai for Wallace's safe return and ask him why the angels didn't bring him home more quickly.

He explains that in the battle between light and dark, when people lose their pets they keep energizing the darkness with anger, fear and grief. In this particular campaign for Wallace there was much light and strength generated. Because of this the little dog's soul agreed to let the horrible conditions continue for a while. This enabled more light to be raised to transmute the negativity around animal cruelty. He added that the dognappers would bear terrible karma and we should pray for their souls, too.

Well, maybe we should, but *this* dog isn't going to!

28 November

Apparently, Wallace is perking up and feeling a lot better.

29 November

Andrew is driving down with Wallace for the day. He's a special dog and I'm proud to be his friend. We are lunching at a restaurant on the beach and I'm longing to see him. He jumps out of the car looking a little thinner but otherwise just as he did before. 'How are you, Wallace?' I ask him.

'That was yesterday. Today is today,' he responds and runs off to sniff around an interesting lamppost.

That's true dog wisdom. Live in the now.

Wallace, a special dog

In the afternoon we call in on Elisabeth and find there are cats everywhere. Ben has been to collect the two his father threatened to take to the RSPCA. Both are enormous and fluffy. They sit and look benevolently at me, which is strange but nice. And here is the strange thing, so does Brutus. I wag my tail.

Apparently, Brutus has fallen in love with one of them and is a changed pussy. He's soft and gentle and goes up to her and snuggles. I can hardly believe it.

Love truly can change everything.

Chapter 31

Sugar and My First Sleepover

30 November

Isabel's birthday is approaching and she talks of nothing but her new puppy. However, there's no sign of it despite everyone searching the puppies-for-sale sites. All I can say is that I hope they choose a puppy I like. Sorry, please change that to choose a puppy that respects and honours me. I like to be top dog.

1 December

The search continues. As soon as school is over, Isabel phones about her proposed new puppy but we have no news. Mum is checking the puppy sites in our area yet again.

2 December

Isabel's mum has seen a puppy advertised and they are going to see it tomorrow, but it's a long way from their house. Mum looks at it on the Internet and gasps in horror. It looks like Dobby in Harry Potter, with a long mournful face and droopy ears.

She says, 'That dog would be more nervous and anxious than you are, Venus. It wouldn't survive two minutes in that household. Besides which it's downright ugly and miserable looking.'

I can't help a little doggy snigger.

Mum asks the angel to help them find the right puppy for Isabel before they buy Dobby. She also extends her search on the Internet and sees a beautiful Cavachon (Cavalier King Charles Spaniel mixed with Bichon Frisé) ready for a new home. She e-mails the details quickly to Lauren and Isabel, and prays that they go to see it.

3 December

We phone to wish Isabel a Happy 10th Birthday. Why do people have to sing tuneless songs down the phone at birthdays? But even I can feel the excitement and I'm not even on the receiver. They are driving after school to see the Cavachon first, then Dobby. The dogs are a long way apart.

At six o'clock Isabel rings. 'We've seen them both and I can't decide. *You've* got to choose, Granny'. I see Mum smile with relief as she says that they seem lovely dogs, but she feels the Cavachon would be the right puppy for Isabel.

However, the universe isn't going to make it that easy! We hear later what happens. The family retrace their route to pick up the Cavachon and are five minutes from the house when their mobile rings. The sellers say that there's been an emergency and they have to leave their home now, so there will be no one there to hand it over. On the scale of disasters, this registers ten on the Richter scale!

The family drives home tired and distraught, without a puppy.

Later the owner phones to apologize and offers to meet them halfway with the puppy.

'What's the lesson?' I ask my angel. She sighs. 'You create what you believe in. If you believe in betrayal, you create betrayal. If you believe in tragedy, it will be set up in your life... And if you believe in drama, it finds you.'

4 December

The puppy is handed over in a garage forecourt.

Isabel phones in ecstasy. It's to be called Sugar. It's robust, friendly and delightful and is sleeping in her bedroom. She manifested her puppy. Well done, Isabel!

7 December

We are on our way to see the new puppy. I hope it's cute – but not too cute!

Sugar runs to greet us at the door and she's sweet. She's eight weeks old and a ball of black and white fur. Sugar is a pretty name, not quite as important-sounding as Venus of course, but it suits the Cavachon because she really is good-natured. We sniff each other contentedly and play all around the garden together.

When we come indoors Mum gives each of us a dental chew. I don't like Sugar having one because, as I'm the older dog, they should both be mine, so I gnaw one and keep my paw over the other one. I growl when she tries to get it, but then I cannot believe my eyes. That puppy takes no notice whatsoever of my senior position or warning growl. She just picks up the chew from underneath my paw and runs off with it. Well, I can't have that. What about my dignity? So what's a girl to do? I run over to her, grab the other end of the chew and we have a pretend tug-of-war. Pretend, because of course I'm much stronger than she is, so I have to be gentle. She's just a baby.

I decide she's a plucky little thing and we can have some fun together, so we race madly around the house into all the rooms, over the furniture, chasing each other and barking. I think that when she's a bit bigger and looks less like a puffball and more like a dog, we could be friends.

In some ways it's good to have Sugar there. Usually, I get into trouble for frightening the guinea pigs and so it's rather nice to have someone I can chase with impunity.

Sugar

8 December

Tonight the family is going to see Pudsey, the performing dog, in Dick Whittington. I think *Uh oh! I bet they have me trying a million tricks tomorrow.* I'll probably be expected to walk on my hind legs or do even more tiresome things.

They do come back and rave about Pudsey and the whole show, but they don't make me do tricks. After the debacle of the agility course, I'm not sure that I want to do anything clever.

10 December

Mum has to go to London tonight and I'm having my first sleepover on my very own at Buddy's. Kathy puts my basket into her car with a whole rucksack full of goodies that Mum has packed for me. She even takes Mum's shawl, but I won't need that. I'm not really a puppy any more.

I jump into the car wagging my tail. I'm going to have a great time. At Buddy's we race around with their friend's dog, who is also a Maltese. Kathy presents my food pouch with a sprinkling of grated cheese for supper and I eat it all.

The problems start at bedtime. They plan for me to sleep in my basket next to Buddy. Big mistake. There's a guinea pig in the same room! I'm part Jack Russell and I won't leave it alone. I couldn't be expected to, could I?

So Kathy puts me in the kitchen. Well, what timid little Papillon-mix terrier would stay in the kitchen in a strange house on her own? I bark and bark. After ten minutes Kathy comes down. She doesn't know what to do with me, so at last she says, 'All right. I'll just have to take you up to my bedroom.' Great! I shoot ahead of her upstairs and straight onto her bed. Okay, not on the bed! She puts my basket on the floor and I cuddle down into it, while she heaves a sigh of relief.

But she's rather surprised in the morning to find me snuggled under the duvet next to her with my little black nose on the pillow beside her. She laughs when she sees me and gives me a cuddle, then we get up. She tells me she's never slept with a dog before, but she doesn't know what she's been missing. She gives Buddy and me some gourmet ham for breakfast, then drives us home to see Mum.

So my very first sleepover is a big success – for me anyway.

15 December

It's the Christmas party at puppy class today. We play party games and I win most of them – and Mum, too, I suppose. That's because we're both competitive. I like musical mats. When the music stops I have to sit on a mat and there's always one fewer mat than competitors. It gets very exciting. There are only two of us left in the game. Buddy and me. We race for the last mat and both sit down quickly. I win because Buddy starts jumping up and down on top of me. For some bizarre reason everyone is convulsed with laughter. I can't imagine what they find funny as I think he's rather a nuisance, but I get a treat.

20 December

You wait weeks for a rabbit and two come at once. It seems to be the same with sleepovers. I'm having another one with Buddy. When Kathy and Buddy come to collect me, Mum and I are waiting for them in the road. I race after Kathy's car and jump into it while Mum collects my basket and things.

What a wonderful time I have with Buddy! However, he's *my* friend and I growl at his other dog friend, Millie, when she comes to play. I try my best to get her to go home and leave

Buddy and me to play, but she can't take a hint. Best of all I sleep in Kathy's daughter's room. I'm a dog who knows my own mind. It's called clarity and is a much prized quality.

Tomorrow Buddy and I are going to have *fun*!

21 December

Kathy and her daughter take Buddy and me to the beach and we see an enormous violet Orb. They find this exciting, though I see them all the time. I get a special reward from the universe as we return to the car park because there's some fox pooh on the ground and I manage to roll in it before anyone can stop me. I bring my own brand of doggy-heaven scent into the car and it's a pity they say, 'Oh, Venus!' quite like that and open all the windows on the drive home. It's even more of a shame that they bath me in the utility-room sink. But that's humans, for you. They don't know a good smell when they're presented with one.

22 December

Isabel phones to say that she wants a horse for her 13th birthday!

Chapter 32

Christmas and New Year

23 December

I'm helping Mum put up the Christmas tree in the lounge this year. She says I'm an invaluable assistant, as I drag lights out of the box and drape tinsel over a chair. I even pull a bauble off a branch – not on purpose, it just falls off when I nudge the tree while chasing Ash-ting. I don't know why Mum keeps laughing and saying how did she manage without me.

Unlike me, Ash-ting is being a pest, deliberately jumping up on the tree and almost knocking it down, so he gets shut out of the sitting room.

When Christmas preparations are fun it raises the energy of the festive season. My presence has lit up the house. I think everyone should have a puppy!

24 December

We are waiting for our visitors to arrive – only two families this year. Now I'm older I quite enjoy seeing them all, though I prefer it when it's not en masse.

They are here. It's that familiar chaos again, but luckily for me everyone is focused on Sugar, who really is a pesky puppy.

She forgets her training in the excitement and does things that puppies do all over the kitchen and conservatory floors. It's not safe to walk anywhere. There are lots of groans and ugh sounds!

Sugar looks up to me as I'm older. I'm definitely top dog.

Taliya is walking now, which is even more dangerous than crawling, but she's a real sweetie and somehow I'm not terrified of her any more. The older children play ball with me in the garden. I wonder if I'll get any bed space tonight?

25 December

It's Christmas Day! How strange – everyone seems to have got up in the dark and they are walking round in dressing gowns, eating bits of toast or bowls of cereal. A very extraordinary thing has happened. Apparently Father Christmas came to the house during the night and left lots of presents for the children. What a generous man! But whose father is he anyway? He must have been very quiet because I have incredibly sharp hearing and pride myself on being the best watchdog in the world. But there are certainly more parcels under the tree this morning than there were yesterday. I hope he's brought me something.

For a minute I wonder if I'm going to get my breakfast, but that kitten meows for England, so Mum says, 'Alright Ash-ting. I'm getting it,' and she feeds all of us animals.

Sharing a bowl at Christmas

Ash-ting and Sugar share a basket

It's a strangely exuberant morning with Sugar and myself tearing up wrapping paper and barking with excitement, while children squeal with pleasure and adults say things like, 'Who gave you that jigsaw? It's not on my list.'

There are lots of presents for Sugar but there isn't even one for me! How can that be? I give Mum a dirty look, but she's too busy to notice. Oh relief, there's just one parcel left under the tree and it has my name on it. Isabel has bought me a squeaky toy! I wag my tail in delight. Someone loves me after all.

In the afternoon Mum, Finn and I, with a little help from Sugar, burn all the Christmas rubbish in the garden. It's very exciting to see all that paper go up in big orange flames, but I stay very composed so that the salamanders will stay calm.

27 December

We are all going to visit a friend today. When we arrive at her house I rush in to see her and wait with my tail wagging for my bit of chicken, because she always has some for me. But she's cooing over that sweet little fluffy baby, Sugar. Grrr! Eventually, she gives me something delicious called turkey. I love her.

We walk over the lawn to the end of the garden where her cabin is. In front of it there's a pond and we are about to cross the bridge when a very large red and silver fish jumps out of the water, looking as if it's about to attack me. I leap back in terror and flatly refuse to step onto that bridge. They go over without me and eventually I find a way round on another path. I will never go over that dangerous crossing again.

Isabel is going to stay with our friend while we go to the beach. She's keeping the puppy with her and I hope Sugar behaves very badly.

We drive to the beach. Oh wow! Those waves are enormous and there are strange men in black doing something called kite surfing. The men in black seem to fly with huge sails, then they flop down into that grey sea and it eats them up. I watch in horror, hoping the sea will spit them out again. I don't suppose they taste very nice because they all come back.

And Finn is so brave! He rushes towards the moaning, crashing ocean which is charging up the beach to attack him. I try to keep it away by barking at it, but it's foaming at the mouth in its rush and he doesn't even have time to take his shoes and socks off before it tries to engulf him. Mum says, 'What is it about seven-year-old boys and water?' and they laugh. But I think he's most courageous. He's quite cold after trying to beat back that water, so we go back to our friend's house. Isabel is all smiley and unfortunately Sugar behaved extremely well. She just would, wouldn't she! But not as well as me, of course. I was protecting Finn on the beach.

28 December

It's more fun than I expected having Sugar to play. Rather to my surprise she can run nearly as fast as I can now. I have to put on my turbo-jet accelerator a few times to get away from her. We play lots of tug-of-war, too. She's very good at giving me something like a toy and then we pull together. That puppy has no fear. If I'm playing with something, she has no qualms about grabbing it so the two of us can tussle.

Sugar and I have a tug-of-war

Afternoon

Sugar's gone. And the rest of the family, too. I do miss Sugar a bit, but strangely enough Ash-ting doesn't want to sleep on the bed any more. It will be rather nice to get an undisturbed night's sleep.

30 December

We are visiting elderly relations today so we get up really early for a long walk in the forest before setting out. I even find something odorous to roll in and I get really muddy. The bath in the sink is the first bad thing of the day, but then I see Mum put a packet of salami in my rucksack. Yum.

The relatives have pale carpets and are nervous of an animal visitor. Also some dogs lie on the floor, but not this one. I'm a chair canine. They keep shooing me off the furniture. Mum tries to persuade me to sit on her knee, but not today, thanks. When lunch is ready they troop into the dining room, leaving me lying innocently on a rug. As soon as they disappear I find Mum's rucksack, which she has obligingly left open. I soon grab the pack of salami, tear it open and consume it all. Then I have a nice comfortable snooze on the sofa until they return from lunch. Knowing me very well, Mum is the first to hurry into the sitting room and quickly yank me onto the floor. She hasn't discovered the salami has gone yet and she still thinks I'm a wonderful, good dog.

We go for a walk.

When we return Mum finds out. I look at her anxiously but she laughs and says, 'You're getting as bad as Ash-ting!'

We leave the elderly relations and drive home.

31 December

It's New Year's Eve, the last day of this year.

We're supposed to be going for a walk with some friends and their dogs. Mum pulls the curtains and says, 'Oh Venus, it's raining cats and dogs.' What! I shoot out from under the duvet and race to the window. Cats and dogs! Are they big or small? Tabbies, white cats, little dogs like me or Alsatians? How exciting. I can't wait.

To my disappointment there are no cats or dogs. Just rain. But Mum wouldn't lie to me, so I think that perhaps the animals are at the back of the house. I race downstairs to the back door but it's just the same. Nasty, heavy, rain. What could Mum have been talking about? I won't believe her next time, even if she says it's raining fish and frogs. In fact, I won't believe anything she says ever again.

In the end we go for a walk on our own, and it's wet and muddy and there are hardly any dogs to play with. Even

Ash-ting refuses to put his nose out of the door. If Mum had told the truth perhaps the sun would have shone.

1 January

Today is the first day of the New Year. I'm told that it's going to be a better one than last year for most people, – once they have integrated the new energy. Apparently, higher-frequency light is pouring into the planet and this shines onto all the stuff that hasn't been cleansed in people's auras. I contemplate this. Perhaps it's like people wearing a white T-shirt on a sunny day, when the sun shows up all the stains. You just have to wash them out.

The sun is shining and Mum smiles, 'That's a good omen for this year.' We set off for a long walk in the forest and I'm on the lookout for omens too. First, Mum splodges in a deep puddle and splashes dirty water all over me. She says it's an accident. Next, a big dog with great floppy paws rushes up to me. Its owners tell me it's only eighteen months old and playful. Well, I'm twenty months old and scared, so I squeal loudly and they haul it back by the collar before it gets a chance to get too near me. Oh no, that's two bad things already. I scuttle along looking for a third message from the universe – and hooray! There's some lovely fox pooh to roll in, then a pile of really fresh and delicious horse pooh to eat. And then, to my amazement, a little white feather glides slowly down from the sky and lands right by my paw. Now I know it's going to be a great year.

Mum looks out for little white feathers all the time, as they are sent by the angels to encourage us and remind us of their presence.

Chapter 33
Rain and Floods

4 January

To our amazement in this freezing wet weather, there's a tent pitched by the path near the entrance to the woods. In fact, it's right where the dogs do their business, which is rather unfortunate. I've never seen a tent before and I bark voluminously, as if it's an invader from outer space.

Everyone is talking about it. Some people think it must be a thief casing the area, or an escaped prisoner. The buzz in the woods is that it isn't safe. All the ladies who live on their own nearby are nervous. I imagine the winter camper must be some sort of giant with a red face and long black hair.

Why aren't all the people nearby asking Archangel Michael to protect their homes?

5 January

The camping person has moved his tent away from the dog pooh onto the other side of the path. As we pass he's outside his tent. He has a beard and a bicycle, and I bark frantically as you would expect. To my horror Mum decides to talk to him. She finds out lots of things, such as he likes camping in the rain and doesn't mind the fact that it's freezing. He doesn't have a home but cycles around visiting friends and relatives. He goes to the supermarket daily to buy fresh water and food. He loves Dorset and likes these woods, in particular.

Mum says he sounds very pleasant and not to be scared of him. What does she mean? She's meant to be scared and I protect her.

6 January

The tent is still there but we don't see the camping stranger. I don't even bark today.

7 January

We meet the camper, wheeling his bike towards the road. He has packed up and says he's on his way. We wish him luck and a good journey, and wave goodbye. He's clearly happy for his aura is a beautiful green, the colour of nature. When people have green auras that shade, they are in tune with the elemental kingdom and are often healers. It just shows you can't judge people just because they may be different from you.

8 January

It has been pouring with rain. I have never seen the roads or the paths in the woods so flooded. This isn't good because Mum expects me to sit before I cross the road and I hate sitting on a wet pavement. However, I've cottoned onto something really clever. I bob my bottom twice and that's to tell her I know what she wants and would sit if there wasn't a puddle there. If I only did it once she might not believe me, so I do a double bottom bob and that works for her when it's raining!

Mum says that when it comes to crossing a road, I've got the brains of a pea. That's a very strange thing to assert. I know what a pea is. It's small and round and is a green vegetable. I'd like to talk to a pea and find out what its brain is like. All the peas we have are frozen ones and don't have much life in them. Also, they don't seem to want to talk to me. Perhaps I'll have to wait until the summer when they are growing in the garden. Then do I address one pea or do I talk to the whole pod? Well, we'll see in the summer, but I'm absolutely convinced I have more brains than a pea.

Now I do admit that if there's a cat on the other side of the road, I would run straight across it, but that doesn't mean to say I'm pea-brained, just cat-focused.

14 January

An old friend of Mum's is coming to stay, so we go to collect her at the coach station. Mum and I are early so we walk in cold, dishwater-grey rain around the car park. How miserable can life get? Eventually, the coach roars in like some yellow monster. I don't bark at Felicity because I recognize her, even though I was just a puppy last time she visited.

But a strange thing happens. Usually people love me the most but she and Ash-ting have formed a special bond. She strokes Ash-ting until he's catatonic. While she strokes him for hours he lies there on his back looking as stiff as a corpse, but really he's stretched out in pure bliss. I wish it was me!

Ash-ting catatonic with bliss

15 January

We go to the beach and have a glorious walk, finishing with hot chocolate at a café. Well, Mum and the others do. I get cold water. At least I'm vibrantly healthy, especially as she blesses the water, so all the dogs who drink from that bowl get a spiritual energy boost.

16 January

We go back to the beach again and I really enjoy it despite the fact that they make me wear my violet-coloured coat. Everyone says, 'Oh Venus, how smart you are.' They don't seem to realize that I'm a dog. I don't care how I look. It's what's *inside* that counts.

17 January

Felicity is leaving today and I've just got to know her, so I don't want to say goodbye. Ash-ting is as devastated as a cat can be. He has never basked in such love before. He's meowing piteously.

I accompany them in the car to the coach station. Halfway there Felicity exclaims, 'I've left my handbag behind!' Mum does a U-turn with alacrity around the next roundabout, saying it's the most terrible thing for a woman to be parted from her handbag. We race home, asking the angels to make sure we are in time for the coach.

When Felicity jumps out to fetch her bag I leap out, too, ready for a game! I'm sure it's time to play. I dodge around the front garden while Mum tries in vain to catch me. Felicity has retrieved her bag, but they can't leave me in the front garden, which opens onto the road and they have only five minutes to get that bus. Mum dashes through the side gate into the garden and I follow her, expecting to play ball. To my shock she nips back through the gate again, shutting me in the garden on my own – in the cold!

When she arrives home I'm shivering on the doorstep, feeling very sorry for myself. Mum assumed I would bark to be let in. Bark in the garden? Me? Never! Mum comments to me. 'Thank goodness for the angels. Felicity caught the coach by the skin of her teeth.' You learn something every day. I didn't know teeth had skin. And what has tooth skin got to do with angels? But I'm glad she caught her bus.

18 January

Mum tries to put that violet coat on me again. I do a runner as soon as I see it, but there aren't many places to escape to in the kitchen, and she soon grabs me and manages to get me into it. My tail is right down to make sure she knows I don't want to wear a coat, let alone a violet one. Luckily it's wet in the woods and when I splash about in muddy puddles she pulls it off me. Joy is freedom from violet coats!

19 January

If the other day was raining cats and dogs, today it's raining elephants and giraffes. I have never seen anything like it. The puddles are enormous and I have to triple dip in the water by the road just to make sure Mum doesn't try to make me sit down before we cross.

There are floods everywhere. I'm glad Mum and I don't live near a river.

20 January

I don't believe it. Mum has had a call from Andrew to say that his house is flooded. Everything on the ground floor and basement is under water. He and Wallace have had to move out of the house again and once more everything is ruined. Another catastrophe! Is his soul aiming to make his aura even brighter?

I can't help wondering how poor old Wallace is feeling. It's all very well being a strong terrier, but he needs a stable home. It's a good job he's got Andrew to comfort him.

And Andrew can't be feeling too good either, I suppose, so I'm glad he's got Wallace. I'm sure if something happened to Mum I'd be the best support in the world. That's what dogs do best.

21 January

It's still deluging with rain this morning, so Mum, Ash-ting and I stay in bed late. It seems everyone has the same idea. At lunchtime the forest is full of moaning people in Wellington boots with macs and umbrellas.

Two men are plodding along in black, hooded raincoats. Help! They look like the spectres of ancient monks and I bark to Mum not to walk along that path. Suddenly I recognize their dogs. Those men always give me treats. I do a U-turn and run after them with my tail wagging. Sure enough they give me tidbits.

All the regular dogs who walk in the plantation encourage treat-giving. It works like this. Someone gives me a biscuit and Mum reciprocates by giving their dog one. Of course, if she gives another dog a treat, she has to give me one, too. Cool, isn't it? Sometimes I don't need breakfast when we get home.

Anyway, the discussion with the men turns to how dirty the dogs get in the forest and whether or not they need a bath when they get home. Mum says she doesn't give me a bath very often. She just rubs me down with a towel. One of the elderly men says that he has a big, thick towel warming on the radiator all ready to wrap his dog in when they go inside! Do I hear right? A big, thick warm towel! You should see the threadbare old thing Mum dries me in. I don't get it warmed on a radiator either. It's not fair. Where's the dog trade union? I want a big, thick warm towel, too.

When we arrive home I get rubbed down with my thin rag, then I stretch out on the sofa. Ash-ting lies on top of me, warming me up as he purrs and licks me. I bet that other dog doesn't get that! Real love is the best kind of warmth.

Chapter 34

Snow

22 January

They say it's going to snow tomorrow. Snow? What's that? Everyone seems very excited.

Mum's daughter Dawn phones and says she has bought a sledge for the girls.

23 January

I wake up to a strange, silent feeling. The kitchen is dark because the adjoining conservatory has a weird blanket over it. Ash-ting and I look out of the window and the grass is white. How peculiar! The trees have turned white, too, and the sky is yellow grey. Even odder, the rain is white. This strange white cotton-wool covering reaches right up to the back door. When Mum opens it Ash-ting and I rush forward eagerly and then stop dead.

Mum announces, 'You'll have to go out for a wee.' I sniff this snow stuff, then stretch out one tentative paw. It sinks right through it. I jump back into the kitchen in shock.

Ash-ting looks at me with big eyes and I think, 'I'm the big one. You're only a kitten,' so I put two paws into the snow and then step gingerly through it to the lawn. Suddenly I realize it's fabulous stuff. I scamper round and round the hazel cluster in the middle of the garden, kicking up the snow.

Because I'm so brave and daring, Ash-ting follows me. Soon he's jumping and sliding and playing with me! Then we chase each other round the trees. Oh this is wonderful! I return inside first, but that kitten simply doesn't want to come in.

Soon Mum says, 'It isn't going to stop snowing, so we may as well go for our walk now.' I wag my tail enthusiastically to indicate I'm ready.

Then she gets out my new violet coat. That's definitely a step too far. She chases me round the kitchen in vain. In the end she holds up the coat and with a chuckle says, 'First catch your dog!' She puts it back in the drawer. Hooray! Victory to me.

There are only two car tracks in the snow. And children are throwing balls of this cold white stuff at each other. What on earth for?

Apparently there's no school today. 'What!' says Mum, 'One inch of snow and the schools are closed!' She says it in inches because she's old. I would say two and a half centimetres of snow.

It's fabulous in the forest. Mum is walking along in a reverie, murmuring, 'Isn't it lovely. Archangel Gabriel has been busy purifying everything.' She's so dreamy she forgets to let me off the lead, but I have my ways of reminding her and soon I'm running as fast as I can through the snow, enjoying a marvellous coat-free time. Some cheeky people are saying that I look off-white against the brilliant white snow. Think I care?

All the old people are sharing stories of how they walked to school through blizzards and had paraffin heaters and had to chop wood for fires. I'm glad I decided to be born now!

On the way home a woman and two children are standing near a huge scary monster. In panic I rush forward and bark loudly to warn them of the terrible danger that is about to strike, but they all laugh and Mum chuckles, 'Venus, it's a snowman.' I'm not at all sure about that, so I approach it cautiously and sniff. I admit it doesn't smell very dangerous, but you can't be too careful.

Someone is coming to our house for a meeting this morning. He phones to postpone, saying that the main road is closed due to fallen trees, and it seems that there has been three inches of snow, with more on its way.

Mum says that perhaps they were right to close the schools after all.

Later

There's still snow on the ground and it's dark and bitterly cold out there. Mum comes home late from an evening event and I tell her that Ash-ting is outside. I'm desperate to bring him in, so Mum opens the back door for me but I can't find him. I run round and round the garden. She goes out several times to call him, too, but no Ash-ting. I'm very worried. Mum leaves a piece of salami on the doorstep, thinking that will bring him in – but no sign. In the end Mum goes to bed. She says the new lodger will let him in later but I don't trust that. I won't go upstairs with Mum. I sit on the mat by the door and bark. I'm shouting, 'Mum come down! Ash-ting is outside!' I can't settle while he's out in the cold. He's not just any cat. He's *my* cat and this is the first time he's stayed out at night.

Mum comes down in her dressing gown and lets me out again. In my haste to rescue Ash-ting I jump straight over his piece of salami without eating it, and run right around the garden three times but he still isn't there. Mum calls me in and this time I can't resist it – I eat his salami. Mum says it's bedtime now, but I'm very worried about my kitten.

24 January

You know what? Ash-ting stays out all night. His first night out all by himself is in the bitter cold.

I rush downstairs and there he is, on the doorstep meowing for his breakfast. He doesn't care that I have had a sleepless night.

Someone suggests my feet might be cold in the snow and Mum should knit me some woollen socks! Oh no! Don't encourage her. That coat is bad enough. I'd be the laughing stock of Dorset if I wore woollen socks.

We come back from a very icy walk in the woods and Mum makes herself a cup of hot chocolate with mountains of cream on top. She says, 'And here's yours, Venus.' I think, *What? Dogs can't eat chocolate or sugar!* but she gives me a bowl of fresh water. I wonder what hot chocolate tastes like? Actually it sounds yukky and it's poisonous for canines.

Mum's friend Carol's dog, a big fat Jack Russell, is really off-colour and drinking all the time. Carol is very worried and doesn't know what's wrong.

She phones to say she's discovered that the dog has sneaked into her daughter's room and eaten all her Christmas chocolates. The vet says there's nothing he can do and a less robust dog would have died. She must keep him drinking.

25 January

Carol says her dog has leaped out of his basket as right as rain. It just goes to show a good constitution is a life-saver.

26 January

As we walk to the shops, with the snow glistening in the sun, we meet the plump postman wearing long trousers. I've never seen him without juicy, tempting bare legs before. Some people always find something to moan about and he's one of them. He's complaining how hard it is to trudge through the snow. It's worse than walking through sand, he tells us.

I listen and don't bark at him once. Afterwards I wonder why? Do I bark at his shorts? Does the snow disguise his scent? Is it because he's not in our road?

My angel suggests it's because I'm maturing into a spiritual dog and am therefore more tolerant and accepting. She doesn't often get things so wrong.

At bedtime I stay in my basket. I don't run upstairs excitedly with Mum as I usually do. To my surprise she shrugs, 'All right Venus, if you want to stay down here in the kitchen with Ash-ting, that's fine.' And she marches off to bed.

I sprawl downstairs

I'm rather upset but think, *You wait. You're going to miss me.*

27 January

To my shock Mum bounces down bright-eyed and alert, 'Hello, Venus. Hello, Ash-ting,' she greets us, as if nothing is different. 'I really enjoyed my night in my own bed on my own.'

I think, *Oh dear, perhaps she won't want me any more! Did I overplay my hand?*

28 January

The instant Mum turns off the television and potters around ready for bed, I race upstairs. I'm lying on our duvet waiting for her when she comes into our room. She smiles.

Sometimes you don't realize how lucky you are until you nearly lose it.

Chapter 35

Escape Artist

29 January

What a beautiful, cool but sunny day. In the afternoon Mum decides to do some gardening, so I take the opportunity to wander around the boundary, sniffing and exploring. Oh miracle! I find a hole in the fence. What happens next is all Ash-ting's fault. He's playing on the other side of the boundary, tempting me. I wouldn't have gone on my own.

I crawl through the hole and we chase each other around next door's lawn. Mum comes to fetch me and every time she nearly catches me, Ash-ting deliberately dashes between us so she misses me. He's so fast and we have such a good time! Then I follow Ash-ting through the hedge into the garden two doors along.

Mum scuttles down the road to knock on their door and retrieves me eventually. I have to stay indoors in disgrace for half an hour while she blocks that fox hole with bricks, but luckily for me she's a firm believer in fresh air and can't bear for me to be inside. I'm clever. I sniff and play around her for a while as she pulls up weeds. Then, when she isn't looking, I jump over the fence in another special place I have found. It works! I escape and Mum didn't see where! I'm free.

Ho ho, it's my secret. I run around next door's garden again, but it's a bit boring without Ash-ting so I trot down the side of their house, onto the pavement and back to our gate. I sit there with my tail wagging and bark to be let in. I'm extremely pleased with myself. I have been out on an adventure and Mum hasn't even realized I'm missing.

She's not pleased.

30 January

Mum and the new lodger are in the garden blocking every hole under the fence and moving anything I can jump over. But they don't know my secret escaping place. I try not to grin as I sit and watch them.

31 January

I'm in dire disgrace today. Mum is so angry with me that she's not speaking to me. All I do is jump over the fence again and wander around the streets for a while. But she can't find where I get out.

1 February

At last Mum has realized I'm jumping onto an old tree stump and then through a small hole in the hedge. I don't know why it took her so long to grasp that's how I was escaping. Now she's put a big piece of wire-netting round the stump. 'Well, you won't be going over there again, Venus,' she declares. I pretend to be dejected, but inside I'm laughing. She doesn't know I still have a secret.

I have been keeping an eye on Ash-ting, who comes and goes as he pleases because he can climb up the chain-link fence. Why can't I do that, too?

Mum has decided that I'm bored, so she's doing much more training with me again, and that's enjoyable, but it doesn't distract me from my main objective – freedom.

2 February

Having watched Ash-ting, I run up the chain-link fence putting my paws through the holes like he does and pull myself over the top. Mum doesn't realize that I can do this. I squirm over the wire and escape again, this time into the garden at the back. I haven't been into this one before. Mum is sweeping up leaves and she sees me on the other side. She calls and calls me, but I ignore her and run down the side of that house onto the road.

Passers-by try to stop me but this is my time for adventure. I'm not going to let anyone come near me, so I bark at them all until they back off.

Mum gets out the car and drives round the streets looking for me. She spots me eventually about a mile away from home. I'm perfectly happy, just strolling along, sniffing the smells, enjoying my freedom – which is the right of every creature, I believe. She stops the car, but I won't get in even though she cajoles and calls me. In the end she drives off and I run after the car. She halts again and gets out to persuade me, but I'm not an idiot. I still won't get in. I'm enjoying my sense of power. I want her to come and play.

A lady who lives in this street very kindly goes into her house to fetch some treats, but they aren't going to catch me that easily. They try again and again and I come up close, but not so near that they can trap me. I'm watching for my chance. The next time Mum puts a treat on the ground I nip in and grab it before she can catch me. Ha ha. I won that one. Then I wag my tail defiantly and trot away down the road. What a triumph!

Mum drives on again and this time when she stops and waits she opens her arms and calls me in the way I love, which usually makes me run to her. But not today. Oh no. I look at her steadily but don't move any nearer.

Finally, she gets into the car and drives all the way to the forest. She says it's the only safe place she can access without going on the main road. I run in the middle of the road behind the car all the way. She might be considerate and travel more slowly – it's a long way for a little dog to run fast!

When we reach the woods I race along all my favourite, familiar paths with an enormous sense of achievement and freedom. This time when she calls me I run to her, expecting her to be delighted. To my surprise, instead of being pleased to have me back again, she puts the lead on, drags me back to the car and throws me in to the back seat. She drives home in silence. When we get in she shouts, 'Basket!' in a very stern voice. Well, I slope into my basket for about two seconds and then I jump out and run into the garden again, cheerfully wagging my tail, enjoying a sniff round. 'Basket,' she yells when she notices me. I stay in it until she goes upstairs.

The new lodger has also been driving round the streets looking for me. When he returns and finds me playing nonchalantly with the kitten he shouts, 'Basket.' I lie in there for what seems like a very long time. What's the matter with them? They want to keep me in, but I like adventure and exploration. They should be praising my initiative and enterprise! Instead Mum frowns that I need more training and I'm not going anywhere without being on the lead.

For my dinner Mum opens a tin of lamb… yuk… she knows I hate lamb. Somehow I know she isn't going to say, 'Here's a bit of chicken for my best dog,' or anything like that, so I eat it all up.

Then she gets out the garlic sausage, my favourite food after chicken, and she gives it to Ash-ting. She looks at me coldly and I guess there's no use wagging my tail or asking for anything. I just lie there watching her and chew a stick, trying to look as if I don't care. I hate her.

Mum and the new lodger have been outside all afternoon raising the height of the wire fence. They have completed both sides and they think I can't escape now because there's a slope up to the back fence, which makes that end too high for a dog my size to get over. They finish and congratulate each other on making a good job of turning the garden into Fort Knox. I'll show them, I think. I watch and wait, then I run up the slope at the back, scale the fence and scramble over, just an arm's length from where they stand gawping impotently at me.

I come back eventually.

I'm only allowed into the garden on my lead until Mum can get that bit of fence raised.

3 February

Ben comes over with a friend and they are raising the back fence.
It's now at least six feet high all round and sealed around the
base. Those humans are convinced there's no way I can get out,
but I bet the kitten will show me a way. He's a Houdini genius.

In the evening Mum lets me out without my lead. She
naively thinks it's safe. It's pitch dark and she doesn't know
that I've got another escape hole. When she calls me there's an
empty silence from the garden. She tours carefully right around
the perimeter with her torch, but can't see where I got out.

She runs down the road searching for me and I materialize
from one of the houses like a white ghost dog with a waggy tail.

4 February

Mum watches me like a hawk and this time she sees me escape.
There's a join where the additional wire-netting has been placed
above the original one. They think it's all carefully secured, but I
have found a place where the two pieces of netting haven't been
properly fastened together. I must confess the cat showed me
how to do it. You jump up where the top fence bulges out and
there's just room to squeeze through.

At one o'clock the lady from the house next door but one
knocks on the door and says, 'Your dog and cat are playing in
my back garden.' Mum thanks her and says she'll get us in a
moment. However, we arrive home together just as she's putting
her coat on.

Once more, I'm not allowed out until she's wired the fence
together again.

Innocently we watch

5 February

Mum says my behaviour is getting worse and worse. She's now putting me on the lead in the forest long before we reach the road. She's at her wit's end and declares that I'll have to be on the lead all the time if I continue like this. What she doesn't understand is that it's not entirely my fault. There's something very strange going on.

Chapter 36

The Spirit Dog

6 February

At last Mum realizes what the problem is. As we sit in bed I'm looking from side to side clearly watching someone. She questions me, 'Who's there, Venus?' She doesn't seem to be able to see it. How very strange. Then it runs out of the room and I jump off the bed to follow it downstairs. She's even more bemused.

She follows me down to the kitchen and then she, too, glimpses it – a spirit dog – a big Jack Russell, much bigger than I am. It's white with some dark brown patches. She says to me, 'Oh Venus, there's a spirit dog in the house. He's been leading you astray.'

I look at her innocently.

7 February

Mum tells her friend Tamsin about the spirit dog. She responds, 'I bet Venus picked it up in the woods.' She adds that I would attract spirits because I have quite a bright light. I'm flattered by this and she's right – I'm a lightworker dog – and it's nice when someone acknowledges it. I wag my tail. I like Tamsin.

Mum realizes that the spirit dog must have attached itself to me when I was terrified by the dog that attacked me. My fear opened my aura and let the spirit dog in.

But then Mum adds with a frown, 'But how did the dog get through the protection around this house?'

'I bet Venus's fear also let the spirit dog through the protection and it's been influencing her to be naughty.'

'And it's been a lot of fun,' I whisper, but they don't register this.

That spirit dog has been running wild in the woods for a long time, but he really wants a home and his family back, and he thinks he can get it through me.

In the evening Mum builds a column of light by calling in Archangel Fhelyai, Angel of Animals, and Mother Mary and some other angels to ask them to help the spirit Jack Russell to pass. She sees the spirit dog start to rise up, so she goes to bed. But she doesn't know what I know.

8 February

You won't believe what's happened this time. The new lodger says, 'You know, I think that spirit dog is still here. I saw one this morning. What was the dog you saw like?'

Mum describes it and he responds, 'That's the one I've been seeing.' What a puzzle. Are there two animals? What is going on?

Mum builds another column of light and this time makes sure that the Jack Russell passes properly into the light.

It's a funny thing, but I feel really good this afternoon. Things are very different between Mum and me. When she calls I go to her straight away and we are friends again. She even announces, 'It's like having my good old Venus back,' so I lick her hand.

9 February

This afternoon Mum and I glimpse a young man with dark hair, a blue shirt and dark trousers sitting on the sofa in the conservatory, but he vanishes almost immediately. She doesn't give it another thought. That proves to be a mistake.

10 February

As Mum walks into the Metatron room, we are horrified to see that the gold cloth has been pulled off the chest and the crystals and beautiful angel that were on it are all scattered across the carpet. The kitten couldn't have done it, so who has? Mum replaces the cloth and rearranges the crystals.

The new lodger tells us that in his bathroom all the toilet paper has been pulled off the roll. Mum remembers the young man she saw in the conservatory and shares this information. They decide they had better find out what he wants. I sit with them and hold the energy.

They light a candle and invite the young man to approach them. He arrives immediately and tells them that the Jack Russell is his dog. He followed his pet from the woods into our house and has been searching for him. When his beloved animal's spirit started to rise into the light the first time, the owner saw it and his desperation called his dog back. So when the new lodger saw the Jack Russell the next day, he was still wandering around in the house.

The young man tells us that when his dog really did go to the light, he felt completely alone and now he wants to join him.

He continues that Ash-ting helped him pull the gold cloth off the chest with the ornaments to draw his plight to our attention. That explains it. They did it together! However, he did manage to pull the toilet paper off the roll himself.

Mum, the new lodger and I call in the angels to send him on his journey. He's ready and when he sees the light he leaves immediately. Now he's with his dog and his family in the light, where he should be.

Anyway, I have got my house back to myself again – and I'm not feeling any desire to escape. Phew!

11 February

Everything feels back to normal. Mum cuts up lots of chicken and hides it around the garden for Ash-ting and me to play 'find'. We watch her from the window and when she opens the door we race out like greyhounds after a rabbit. I'm the winner. I find twelve chicken treats and Ash-ting only gets three. That's not bad for a kitten, I suppose, but why should he get any? I have to do training exercises for my treats while that cat just meows and meows and Mum gives him treats for doing nothing. I think that's grossly unfair.

My angel reminds me that every creature incarnates with a different purpose. 'Even those who get treats without doing anything to earn them?'

'Yes.'

Ash-ting gets treats for doing nothing

I sigh. I'm trying to accept Ash-ting exactly as he is. I can't imagine what his purpose is.

I don't like vegetables and I never have. I will not eat anything green or orange. I have a very good nose and I can push them out of my bowl. Mum often tries to secrete bits of broccoli and even grated carrots in my food. But today I did accidentally eat a pea. Mum put it on a low table and said, 'Find.' Of course, I rejected it every time she did this. Then Ash-ting raced over to see what I'd got. He was just about to grab it, so I gobbled it up quickly!

Perhaps Ash-ting's purpose is to encourage me to eat green vegetables.

Chapter 37
Sugar Visits

12 February

Isabel and Sugar, who is four months old now, are staying. How that puppy has grown! We have a wonderful time racing around the house and garden. However, she's not at all house-trained and I can't believe I was really like that once! Was I?

When we come in from our walk, Isabel showers the poor creature. She's no dirtier than I am, but Isabel likes to keep her immaculate. Sugar doesn't mind being drowned in water and shampoo, while I go berserk before, during and after a bath.

My friend Buddy, too, is washed almost every day. He's always gleaming white and could be a male model. Ugh! It would drive me nuts.

Buddy is always gleaming white

I obviously got the right owner for me as Mum is much more casual, though she does draw a line when I roll in fox poo. She doesn't like sleeping with a smelly fox.

As usual Isabel insists on sleeping in my bed with Mum and me – and where she goes Sugar has to go, too. That Sugar has no shame. She bounces onto my side, cocky as you like, as if she owns it. I have to sleep on top of the duvet because there's no room under it. Isabel sleeps like a starfish and keeps kicking out, so I'm knocked clean off the bed several times in the night. Mum has to curl up in a ball in one corner.

To make it worse, Ash-ting, who usually goes out at night, now insists he's sleeping in our bed, too.

And there are another seven nights to go! Will I survive?

Mum says I can sleep in my upstairs basket. What, and miss the fun of being with everyone! She simply doesn't understand.

13 February

We take Sugar with us to the Platinum Class. Of course the class is for advanced dogs like me, but she's very good. She isn't in the least fazed by all the Labradors and golden retrievers who are just enormous in comparison to her. I do everything perfectly, such as walking round the posts, then completing a figure of eight off the lead. Our trainer allows Sugar to do some exercises, too, and she does them all beautifully – rather to my surprise. I'm quite proud of her, a feeling encouraged by the fact that Sugar thinks I'm wonderful.

When we go out Isabel dresses Sugar in a pink baby dress and everyone we pass laughs or comments. It's so embarrassing.

Please don't let Mum get any ideas! The odd thing is that Sugar doesn't mind at all and Mum says she's a very amenable puppy. Well, I'm not! I have very clear ideas about my doggy-ness. No clothes or bows for *me*.

Kathy pops round with Buddy and shows us some photos of him in a hat and a sailor suit. 'Isn't he cute?' she says.

'How could you?' I ask him.

He shrugs. 'You know what?' he responds. 'It keeps them happy.'

I look at the humans' beaming faces as they pore over the photos. Could I be wrong? But Mum catches my eye and winks at me. 'There are all kinds of different people,' she whispers, 'and all kinds of different dogs, too. You are strictly a dog's dog!' And she slips me a treat. I sigh with relief.

14 February

This has been the best day of my life! I go to the beach with three of my favourite people, Mum, Isabel and Kathy, and two dogs, Sugar and Buddy. We are three little white dogs, best friends and all exactly the same size, and we race around together. Kathy comments how nice it is when you walk on the beach because you don't have to bath your dog when you get home. Oh, be careful what you say! There's a place below the cliff where a stream pours down and turns into sludge. We dogs decide to play chase through this and we get absolutely covered with thick, oozing, sticky mud.

Isabel tries unsuccessfully to wash Sugar off in the sea. The puppy immediately rolls in the sand and looks like some grotesque clay creature.

We return to the car park in the little train that runs on the other side of the headland. Three people and three dogs cram into a carriage with a man, two children and their black Labrador. I growl at the Labrador because he's too near to me, but when I have established my space, I enjoy sitting on Mum's knee with the breeze blowing in my face.

On the way home we visit the pet shop. Boring! All the people want to do is look at collars and leads! I can feel my energy getting heavy and grey. Then Mum and I walk past the pet section and it smells like heaven. There are gerbils, rabbits, hamsters, rats and mice scrabbling about in cages. Goodbye boredom. I'm so excited! My tail is wagging as if it will fall off and I nearly get through the glass. Amazing how one little mouse can bring so much joy to a dog.

Boredom is grey, while joy and happiness light people up like an orange sun. My angel says the more happiness people build into their lives, the brighter their energy.

Mum buys some new balls and throws them all into the garden for Sugar and me to pick up. I get them all because she's a baby and is much slower than I am. Then I gather them together and guard them so Sugar can't have one. Mum says this is dogs behaving badly and the reason wars start, but I say it's because they are *my* balls and I'm three-quarters terrier.

I think about what Mum says and generously let Sugar have one of the balls. She's pathetically pleased.

15 February

Mum takes Isabel to the stables for horse riding. Little Sugar is nervous of the horses, but I show her how to behave and tell her that if she's quiet they won't hurt her. She doesn't utter a peep. I'm clearly a Master Teacher.

Mum says the only way to teach is by example. Quite right.

We walk in Moors Valley this afternoon, which is miserable – too many screaming children. Enough said. I reiterate that the sooner dogs rule the world, the better. Then dogs will be allowed to bark while children are told off for yelling.

16 February

Kailani, who's now three, and Taliya, who's nearly two, arrive with their parents. I hope Mum and I get some sleep tonight.

Wrong! What a night. The older cousins, Isabel and Kailani, want to sleep together so they make a den of cushions on the floor in the bedroom next to Mum's. Sugar and Ash-ting sleep in bed with Mum and me. Here's how our night goes:

1 a.m. Mum gets up to tend Kailani, who has fallen off the cushions onto the floor and is crying. Mum lifts her back and tucks her in.

1:30 a.m. Isabel wakes and joins us in our bed.

2 a.m. Kailani wakes and joins us in our bed.

2:30 a.m. Sugar jumps heavily off the bed, waking us all, but then jumps back on again.

3:00 a.m. I decide I need a wee and ask to be let out, so Mum creeps out of the bed without waking the children to take me down to the garden.

4:00 a.m. Ash-ting wakes and starts prowling around the bedroom, playing, so Mum gets up and boots him out.

5:00 a.m. Kailani wakes. She sits up and demands a midnight feast. She talks non-stop until 6 a.m.

6:00 a.m. Mum, Kailani and I go down to the kitchen to make a midnight feast. (I know, I know, it's a 6 a.m. midnight feast). They sit on the floor on cushions and I lie beside them. They have smoked salmon, cheese biscuits, apples, pineapple cut into chunks, crisps and orange juice. Kailani loves it.

7:00 a.m. Everyone else gets up.

17 February

The entire family is here today to celebrate Justin's 40th birthday.

They talk about the notorious volcano cake Mum made when he was at school, so we have to hear about it again.

Apparently, when it was their birthday at school the boys' parents sent in cakes. The year Justin was 12, Mum happened to be in England and he asked her to bake him a cake. This is not one of Mum's best skills, but she duly bought the ingredients and made a chocolate cake. It collapsed disastrously in the middle, so she made a second one. The same thing happened. So she spread thick butter icing in between the layers and cut a dip in the top to make it into a volcano. But even drowned in brown icing and decorated with flames of red and yellow icing, it still looked terrible. In desperation, she searched the shops for sparklers and stuck them liberally over it.

She crept into school and put her monstrosity next to the professionally crafted aeroplanes and forts and boats.

Imagine her surprise when she had an ecstatic call from Justin to say that it was the best cake ever – and the headmaster had announced in assembly next day that no boy was ever to have fireworks on their cake again! The imagination runs riot and the family all laugh, as usual.

My angel is laughing, too, and declares that when your intentions are good, the outcome often surpasses your greatest hopes.

We have sparklers on Justin's 40th birthday cake (not baked by Mum) to commemorate the infamous volcano cake.

19 February
They have all left. I do miss Sugar! And the family, of course!

23 February
It's Platinum Class tonight and it isn't until we get into the hall that Mum discovers I've chewed into her bag and eaten all the nibbles, including the salami she has brought as a special treat. 'You noodle, Venus!' she exclaims. I do feel rather full, so I lie down quietly and am extremely quiet.

There's a new young Labrador in the class tonight. He's very naughty and keeps jumping up and refusing to do what he's told. I'm sure I was never like that.

At the end of the evening the adults are asked to swap dogs. No way! Mum has the Labrador puppy and she strokes it a lot. Grrr. I don't take my eyes off her for a moment. I reluctantly go with Bill, the spaniel's dad. The instant he lets me off the lead I charge straight back to Mum. I tell that Labrador off very loudly and crossly for taking treats from my mum. The teacher takes me away.

I like Sally, a little grey-white cocker spaniel. She's very cute, but she never actually does anything right. I don't know how she got her bronze, let alone her silver. Her dad brings her to the class and he keeps making excuses for her.

26 February

We meet Sally, the cocker spaniel, out walking with her mum, who we have never seen before. We dogs greet each other like friends and her mum says it's as if we know each other. My mum hasn't cottoned on yet that the spaniel is Sally, so she listens politely as her owner tells us proudly that she does everything perfectly in her puppy-class lessons. 'My husband tells me Sally is the star of the class,' she adds. I gasp, 'What! I'm the star of the class.'

Mum has suddenly realized who the dog is and is listening open-mouthed. My angel laughingly reminds me that the human capacity for self-delusion is unbelievable.

For a long time Kathy has been talking about getting Buddy neutered and at last the date is set for Monday, so he'll miss our class. He's nearly two years old and I'm pleased it's happening at last, because he won't leave me alone. Even though I've been spayed, I appear to be the most alluring dog in the world to him. If we were humans I'd do him for sexual harassment. Mum is more charitable and says Buddy and I must have been partners in a past life.

On Monday Mum phones to find out how Buddy is after his op. Kathy replies that she couldn't go through with it. 'I decided he's my little man and I love him as he is.'

Chapter 38

Spring Time

28 February

Mum keeps calling me Monkey, recently. 'Come on, Monkey', she says. Or, 'Stop doing that, Monkey'. Is that my new name? I don't know what a monkey is. The grandchildren have toys they call monkeys. They've got long arms and legs, and funny little faces, but I'm not like that. I've got short legs, so she can't possibly be thinking I'm turning into a monkey, can she? I thought my command of human language was getting better, but sometimes I find it very confusing.

She also had a phase of calling me a noodle, which is even odder. This afternoon she pulls me off a wall saying, 'Come down, Venus, you noodle.' I thought noodles were those worms in tins that the grandchildren seem to find palatable. In her wildest imagination she can't think I'm a worm, can she?

4 March

Mum and I are out for a walk when I plunge into a thicket and disappear. I often do this, so Mum continues down the path. After a while she calls me. I'm busy so I don't respond and she carries on calling. I'm chasing a squirrel, so I bark my high-pitched excited bark. Mum returns to where she last saw me and keeps shouting my name.

I'm yapping with excitement at that animal. It's running up one tree and jumping to another. Then it runs along the ground to a third tree and I nearly catch it. I'm so very close. The pesky creature waves its tail at me and races around the same circuit again. Mum doesn't know that I'm barking at a squirrel. She decides I'm in trouble. She thinks I'm caught or trapped. So she walks back along the path and calls me, 'Venus, are you all right?'

'Woof,' I say.

'Venus, where are you?'

'Woof.'

'It's all right, I'm coming to find you.' She crawls through the gorse on little tracks she never knew existed, but I know very well.

'Woof, woof, woof.' That furry tormentor is on the ground again.

'Don't worry. I'll be with you in a moment.'

'Woof.' I miss it. It's up the tree.

'Hold on, darling. I'm nearly there.'

What's the matter with her? I think, and bark again.

The squirrel is on a branch, just out of reach. I bark frantically. I *will* get it. I hear Mum crashing about. She emerges into the clearing where I am. She has twigs in her hair and her coat is full of prickles. I'm standing at the bottom of the tree with my tail wagging crazily with excitement.

'Oh, Venus,' she says. 'What an idiot I am! I thought you were in trouble. Come on.'

She turns and disappears into the thorny thicket again. Something tells me I should leave the chase and follow her. So I do.

5 March

Mum puts on her coat and immediately gets a huge gorse prickle in her arm from that thicket she crawled through yesterday. She looks at me, but she doesn't say anything.

'Let it go, Mum. Let it go. That was then. This is now.'

'You're right Venus,' she smiles. 'You're a good teacher!'

9 March

In one of the isolated parts of the forest a couple we pass tells us that there's a very strange young man sitting on a log further down the path. The husband says, 'If you need any help, just shout.'

Mum laughs and thanks him, then says she's got her trusty wolf to look after her. I puff up. Of course, I'm there to protect her if she needs it.

She places Michael's deep blue cloak around us and when we reach the bench she says cheerfully to the strange young man, 'Good morning, you've got a lovely place to sit.' He's actually very pleasant. He puts his hand out to me and I very gingerly approach him to sniff it. I'm ready to run if he moves, but I would come back to protect Mum if necessary. They chat for some time and I don't even have to bark.

My angel smiles, 'Well done, Venus. Trust others, but use intuition and common sense.'

15 March

We have just met a huge boxer puppy with long legs like a giraffe. It bounces excitedly all over and around me, and I feel very nervous. I growl and tell it off in no uncertain terms, but it takes no notice. Mum shouts 'No!' to it in a stern voice and its mistress hurries up and she too shouts, 'No'. But it is unabashed and has to be put on a lead. Our owners have a long chat and, to my irritation, Mum gives the boxer a biscuit it doesn't deserve.

She says, 'Venus, next time we meet, maybe that boxer will remember the biscuit and be calmer around you.'

20 March

We meet one of the treat-giving men with his two dogs. He's riding a lurid green bicycle, so he stops to explain that he has just rescued it. He tells us that in the swampy part of the forest, which is extra wet because of all the rain, he met a young man who was covered in mud, completely lost and had abandoned his bicycle.

Our kind man gave him directions to get home and took his address. Then he searched the swamp and retrieved the bike. Now he's taking his very muddy animals home before returning the green bike to the lost man's house. My angel reminds me that there are some very caring and kind people in the world. They are accruing good karma by doing generous deeds. She adds that you never know when you might need a good karmic credit in your balance sheet of life, so try to offer random acts of kindness whenever you can.

25 March

Mum takes me for a three-hour walk this morning. It's fabulous. Admittedly, we stop and talk to people and I have a little rest then, but I also race around with all my friends. I'm exhausted when we get home and I immediately fall fast asleep on the sofa. Ten minutes later the new lodger announces, 'I'm going for a walk in the woods. I'll take Venus.' I look at Mum in horror. Not another walk! I bury my head under a cushion and half close my eyes. The new lodger persists, 'Come on, Venus, walk time.' I dig my head in deeper in the hope that he won't see me. Mum laughs, 'I don't think Venus wants another walk yet.'

Phew! The new lodger goes without me. My angel says he's being kind but unaware, and adds that people and animals should always look out for each other. I lick Mum's hand. I'm her dog and I *always* look out for her.

28 March

Oh no! Andrew has just phoned. His house has flooded *again*. It's just the basement this time. How can poor old Wallace be feeling?

I look at my angel, 'What can the lesson be this time?'

She shakes her head, 'Just don't ask, Venus. Just don't ask. If you don't learn the lesson the first time, it keeps coming back to you.'

Mum lights a candle and we ask Archangel Fhelyai, the Angel of Animals, to look after Wallace, and Archangel Michael to be with Andrew.

Sometimes, just asking the angels to help is the best thing you can do.

Chapter 39
I'm Nearly Two Years Old

29 March

I'm nearly two now and I still find life challenging. Ash-ting may love me and curl up with me, but he's ruining my street cred. He always meets us on our return from the forest. He ignores Mum but, in full view of everyone in the street, he runs up to me meowing, then nuzzles my face and snuggles up to me. Rubbing against me he walks beside me all the way home.

This morning a lorry driver actually stops and gets out. He says, 'I've never seen anything like it. It warms your heart, don't it?'

1 April

I still get things wrong occasionally. This morning I'm nearly attacked by dangerous monsters in the forest. We are wandering through the trees when suddenly I hear a terrible noise like thunder, only worse. It reverberates through the ground. I see a cloud of dust and huge creatures are charging down the path towards us. Mum is shouting, 'Venus, come here!' but I ignore her. Those fiends might attack her. Even worse, they might go for me! So I put my tail up and push my fur out until I look as big as a tigress, and race towards them barking hysterically. They slow down as I get near and I see they are just horses. What a relief! One lady rider murmurs, 'Oh, what a sweet little dog!' Grrr. I'm a brave tigress.

2 April

When I was a small puppy I was terrified of the metal cat with large, shiny green eyes in our neighbour's garden. Well, I'm a big grown-up dog now and it can't scare me any more. This evening I glimpse it lurking on their front lawn, menacing me with its emerald eyes. In a trice I jump over the wall, growling and barking loudly and run towards it menacingly. I'll see it off. Mum laughs and I'm quite insulted. Why?

3 April

We are staying with Mum's daughter and the children. Kali Cuddles, Ash-ting's mother, is nearly two now. Their neighbours have spent much of the winter building a pond, of which they are inordinately proud. It has finally been finished and they have ceremoniously filled it with water. This morning they are going to stock it with fish, which they have chosen with great care. Mum warns them about herons, which pillage ponds, and suggests they buy some netting. They laugh.

5 April

At lunchtime we hear shouts from the next-door garden. Sugar and I run to the fence and bark! Mum, Lauren, Isabel and Finn peer over to see what's going on.

Apparently, the family next door are tucking into their lunch, proudly surveying their new pond, when Kali Cuddles flips one of the new fish out with her paw. She proceeds to sit on their lawn complacently eating it before they can intervene. They're not happy.

Kali is now fast asleep, stretched out in the sun, without a care in the world.

7 April

A long time ago I discovered that if I sit in front of Mum, wag my tail, let my eyes shine and look eager, she will give me a treat. It's money for old rope. I do it quite often. She had a period of saying, 'No, you have to do something for it,' but that has passed. It's working again.

She says, 'Ah Venus, you expect a treat, do you?' And she delves into her pocket and gives me one!

It just shows you should never give up.

9 April

Ash-ting is as naughty as ever. Returning from the woods, Mum and I bump into a lady who lives in the next road, with her big black Labrador. Ash-ting naturally comes squealing up to me. 'Hello, hello, it's me, meow!' The lady exclaims, 'Is that your cat?' Mum reluctantly confirms that he is and the woman tells her that he's driving their dog nuts. Apparently, their dog likes to sit in their conservatory and watch out over the patio and garden. Our kitten enjoys playing on their patio taunting him.

He runs up to the window as if to say, 'Ha ha, you can't get me.' The Labrador goes crazy in the conservatory while Ashting wafts his tail loftily in the air and does whatever he can to tease him.

10 April

This morning Mum says I'm lazy. Me, the busiest dog in the world! I must confess that I often stay under the duvet these days, while she does her e-mails and goes on Facebook. What's the point of getting up until she goes downstairs?

This morning someone knocks on the front door and I have to do my duty as a dog, so I bark a few times from under the duvet. She calls that lazy. I call it conserving energy. It's a sign that I'm nearly two years old.

Conserving energy

12 April

I continue to teach Mum all the time. It took her a little time to realize that I refuse to sit on her lap after she has been working with her laptop on her knees. I can feel the electromagnetic energy and I don't like it. She must be learning because now she tends to type at the table with her feet on an earthing blanket.

I also try to teach her just how much energy from television we absorb into our auras. One evening, she watches a rather dark, true story on TV, after which I refuse to sleep on her bed. She will think twice before she watches anything like that again.

14 April

Mum calls me back in mid-flight after a jogger and I stop running!

This afternoon I'm chasing a deer and come back when called. Soon, I will no longer be a puppy. I will be a *dog*.

17 April

We bump into that puggle and his owner for the first time in ages. Is that the little puppy I growled at when he was put on my lead and given my treats? I can hardly believe it. He looks like a big, solid dog. It's good to see him and know he's doing well.

18 April

We see a huge angel cloud in the sky where an angel has watched over the forest. When the angel flew away, the cloud formed over its high-frequency energy.

By mid-morning the rain stops and the sun comes out. We see a rainbow. Ah, my heart leaps with delight. My angel tells me that when you see a rainbow and your heart leaps, you trigger the universe to bring forward a new opportunity for you. I'm waiting and watching!

20 April

Sugar runs around the garden with me and, to my horror, I discover she's faster than I am already. Isabel calls her and she goes to her immediately. Mum calls me and I eventually run inside. There everyone is cuddling and stroking Sugar. She is lying on her back, surrounded by people and squirming with joy. They all say, 'Sugar, you are lovely.'

I don't like lots of people around me, so I go over to Mum. She strokes me and says, 'Venus, you may not be the most obedient dog in the world, or the fastest dog in the world or the friendliest, but you're *my* Venus'.

Life is good. I am happy being me.

22 April

It's my birthday and I'm two years old today. My angels remind me that a birthday is a very special day as it commemorates the day you come to Earth. They say we should celebrate. Mum wakes and says, 'Happy Birthday, Venus,' though thankfully she doesn't sing. Ash-ting wanders in to greet me, jumping onto the bed and snuggling himself against me.

I listen to the birds as they sing in my special day with their dawn chorus. Mum yawns and gets out of bed, then clatters downstairs. Mmm! My nose twitches. Yes, a glorious birthday breakfast of chicken is on its way. Life is wonderful!

'What are the most important things you've learned so far in your life, Venus?' asks my yellow angel.

I nudge Ash-ting playfully with my nose. 'That life is better when we look after each other,' I respond, and my angels nod.

'And?'

I ponder for a moment and think about poor Stray, the cat abandoned as she was about to give birth to Ash-ting's mother.

Yes, the smell of chicken has made me generous-hearted, so I reply, 'I've learned to be compassionate and never to judge because you don't know what anyone's gone through.'

My angels nod, pleased with my response, but they are waiting expectantly for more. Luckily Mum walks in, beaming from ear to ear, carrying my birthday breakfast-in-bed, two bowls of chicken.

I cock my ear towards the angels, 'It's good to share,' I murmur, and they high-five each other in delight. Yes, angels really do this!

Ash-ting puts his head into one of the bowls. What! It's *my* birthday treat. I want them both! As I'm about to push him out of the way, I catch the angels' expressions – and stop. I graciously allow Ash-ting to eat some chicken.

Mum strokes me adoringly. 'You really are the very best dog in the world, Venus.'

I thump my tail happily. Mum and I are in perfect agreement.

I am not a puppy any more. I am Venus, the *dog*. Sometimes, I'm even Venus, the *enlightened dog*.

****

Postscript

John returned from South Africa after his treatment and is now full of health and vitality. There's no sign of cancer in his body.

Annie, Elisabeth's daughter, contacted her and went to visit her. They fell into each other's arms and confessed that it had been terrible not to see each other for so long. They have totally healed their relationship and see each other often.

Andrew has moved back into his house with Wallace.

The new lodger has moved to an ashram in India.

Ash-ting has not followed us to the woods since a large white cat jumped down from a tree and landed right on top of him, squashing him. Luckily, I was nearby and jumped on top of the white cat, squashing them both. A lot of noise and chaos ensued, but Ash-ting emerged unscathed and now waits for us at the end of our road, like a sensible animal.